UXBRIDGE

A Concise History

Carolynne H̲ ̲non
MA, BA, ALA
Local Studies Librarian,
Uxbridge

HILLINGDON BOROUGH LIBRARIES
1982
Revised reprint 1984

CONTENTS

ACKNOWLEDGEMENTS

I wish to acknowledge the assistance of many others in producing this book and of all those who helped to build the very fine local history collection at Uxbridge Library, without which this book would not have been possible: in particular Miss E. J. Humphreys, F.L.A., who nursed the collection for many years whilst she was the Uxbridge Librarian; the knowledgeable Mr. Ken Pearce, B.A., Chairman of the Uxbridge and District Local History Society who has checked the facts; and Miss Mary Pearce, B.A., F.L.A., Local Studies Librarian, who compiled the index.

CAROLYNNE HEARMON

ILLUSTRATIONS

INTRODUCTION

'The study of history is one of the most pleasing, and may be made one of the most instructive of human pursuits.' So begins the introduction to 'The history of the ancient town of Uxbridge' by George Redford and Thomas Hurry Riches published in 1818. "Redford and Riches" has remained the standard work ever since; and now over 160 years later the present book will show that the study of the town's history can still give pleasure and instruction to people of all ages.

Carolynne Hearmon has written this concise history to help the general reader to take an informed interest in the town of Uxbridge: but the serious student will also find in it all the essential sources now brought together for the first time since 1818.

Apart from a time during the Civil War when Uxbridge achieved some fame as a frontier town, it has not been prominent in the great tides and events of history. For centuries it was an important coaching centre and market town, and there are 'Uxbridge Roads' which bear witness to this for miles around. When the railways destroyed the coaching trade and the business of the market declined, it took a long time for Uxbridge to adjust to modern times. When the changes did come they were sudden and dramatic, for the face of Uxbridge has been transformed, not always for the better, over the past twenty years. This book will help some readers to recapture affectionate memories of the town as it was; it will help others to appreciate and understand the town's development into a modern centre.

It is a great pleasure to welcome this long awaited book and to congratulate Carolynne Hearmon on a splendid achievement.

PHILIP COLEHAN
BOROUGH LIBRARIAN

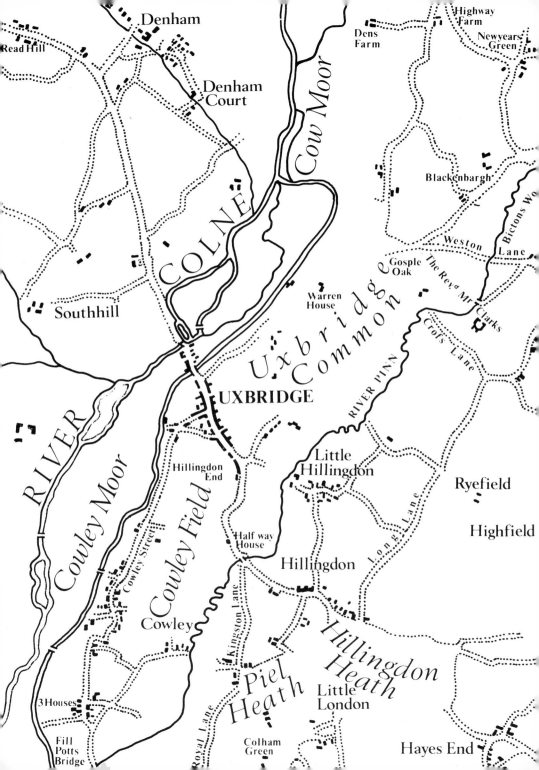

Chapter One

The Origins of Uxbridge

The early history of the district now known as the London Borough of Hillingdon, in which Uxbridge is situated, is very difficult to trace. The only evidence we have is from archaeology. Primitive men did not live in permanent settlements, but led a nomadic existence following the animals which were their prey. They had not discovered the use of metals, so their tools and weapons were made of stone. The earliest evidence of man in this area is from the Palaeolithic, or Old Stone Age. This was during the period of the great Ice Ages, when there were long spells when Northern Europe was covered by ice, interspersed with more temperate periods. This area was never covered by glaciers, but it was affected by the deposits left by the melting ice. These deposits caused the River Thames to keep changing course, laying down the different gravel terraces on which Uxbridge is situated. Archaeologists use these different layers of gravel to date the tools which are found there. At Yiewsley, just over two miles from Uxbridge, a great many Palaeolithic stone tools have been found, making it one of the most important sites in Britain. Such tools have also been found at Hillingdon and Harefield, showing that early man roamed over the whole of this region.

After the ice finally retreated, the basis of the present landscape was laid down. The types of soils and the river systems have remained relatively unchanged, apart from some minor changes in the course and levels of the rivers. At the beginning of the Mesolithic, or Middle Stone Age, the climate was rather cool and damp. At this stage the Colne Valley was a complex system of marsh and fen, interconnecting streams and islands of firmer ground. The banks were heavily wooded with a mixture of oak and beech. The clay hills to the north were virtually impenetrable, with a thick undergrowth of hornbeam, while the lighter soils to the south had a more open forest growth. The people who inhabited these woods 8,000 years ago were nomadic hunters and gatherers; they have left little behind them except a few flint tools found at Uxbridge and Harefield, although they roamed the whole locality.

About 6,000 years ago men discovered how to herd animals and grow crops for food rather than rely on what they could find in the wild. The beginning of farming took place in what is known as the Neolithic, or New Stone Age. Farming led to more permanent settlement sites, and although no early sites have been found in this area some domestic sites dating from the later part of the period have been found near Heathrow, as well as some stone axes and arrowheads found at Uxbridge.

The discovery of the uses of metal had a profound effect on the lives of early men. Metal made their tools and weapons a great deal more effective. The first metal to be used was bronze, and then iron. There is evidence of Bronze Age man in Uxbridge; he also seems to have lived on the lighter soils around

Facing: Map of Uxbridge area based on John Rocque's map of Middlesex, 1754.

Heathrow. By the beginning of the Iron Age, around 500 B.C., the population had become more settled. Once again there is no evidence to show that Iron Age men lived on the site of Uxbridge, but the area around was important. At Harefield, on a hill overlooking the Colne, early Iron Age burials have been found, suggesting that this was the site of a small settlement. Not far away, at Gerrards Cross in Buckinghamshire, is a large Iron Age hill-fort which would have protected the people in this part of the Colne Valley. However, of much more importance is the site at Heathrow. This was both an extensive settlement and an important ritual centre, with a large rectangular wooden temple.

When the Romans arrived in Britain in 43 A.D. the country around the site of Uxbridge was much as it had always been; heavily wooded and thinly settled. The Romans did little to change this. There are no Roman villas in the area and the only settlements were small farms supplying the London market, most of which were to the south of Uxbridge. The area was not left completely untouched, as the Romans may have built some roads in the district. None of the major military routes passed through the district, but there were smaller roads linking towns and villas. A minor road from Staines to St. Albans (Verulamium) is reputed to have passed through Uxbridge on its route up the Colne Valley. From Yiewsley its course would have passed close to the present Cowley St. Laurence Church, along the approximate line of Park Road in Uxbridge, and through Harefield, past Breakspear House, where some Roman sepulchres were found. Cowley Church is interesting in that a church dedicated to St. Laurence is often found near a Roman site, and the dimensions of the church are said to be based on those of a Roman building; but this is pure speculation and there is no archaeological evidence to support it. It is also possible that at this time the importance of the ford across the Colne at Uxbridge was realised. It is highly likely that the Oxford Road is a Roman route to the settlement at High Wycombe, and it would have crossed the Colne near Uxbridge.

The final departure of the Romans in 410 A.D. can have made little initial difference to the inhabitants of the Uxbridge area. However, the Saxon invaders did not take long to penetrate this far. By the end of the fifth century they had reached and begun to settle in this district. The Saxons were sailors and they reached Uxbridge by boat, up the Thames and then the Colne. In its name West Drayton preserves an echo of this, for 'Draeg-tun' means that this was a place where they had to drag the boats a short distance overland. The early settlers chose places with a good light soil and access to water. The heavily wooded clay hills were not settled until later. The leader of the group of Saxons who settled here was probably called Hildric, or Hilda for short. He and his people chose the top of a hill above the Colne valley to which he gave his name; Hilda's Hill, or Hillingdon. The site of Uxbridge was probably still too damp and liable to flood. However, it is possible that there were some people living close to the river to guard the site of the ford. Both Denham and Hillingdon on each side of the Colne are very early settlement sites; the ford and site of Uxbridge are exactly half-way between these two villages.

The Saxons were organised in tribes. Each inhabitant of a village would be a member of the same tribe and they often gave their name to the area in which they lived; Middlesex, for example, was the territory of the Middle Saxons. A small tribe called the Wixan lived in Lincolnshire: some of its members also lived in what is now north-west Middlesex. It is from this tribe that the name of Uxbridge is derived; it means the bridge belonging to the Wixan. The Wixan are mentioned in a seventh century document called the 'Tribal Hidage' and it is reasonable to assume that their bridge (more likely a ford at this time), or at least a crossing point on the Colne controlled by them, was already in existence. The river Colne was an important political boundary; it divided the territories of the Middle Saxons and the Mercians, so control of its crossing was vitally necessary.

For the next five hundred years the Saxons farmed the land and cleared the woodland. The villages they founded are still the main settlement sites in the area, despite the many changes since. The Saxons were basically arable farmers. They ploughed the land to grow crops, pastured their cattle in the water meadows and their pigs in the woods. As the easily ploughed light soils were used up by the growing population they began to clear the previously untouched woodlands. Few outside events disturbed the regular pattern of the farmers' year. From the middle of the ninth century the Viking attacks on England grew fiercer, and under Alfred the Great the defence against them became more organised. In the year 894 a host of Danes, escaping with their wounded leader from a battle at Farnham, crossed the Thames and took refuge on an island in the Colne near Iver, at Thorney. There they were besieged by King Alfred's army until the English ran out of provisions. The Danes then escaped east to Benfleet. The Viking invasions also brought about the creation of Buckinghamshire. This was designed as an area of land allocated to provide support and provisions for the fort at Buckingham, built early in the tenth century. The river Colne was taken as part of the southern boundary of this territory. When creating an administrative structure the Saxons divided the counties into hundreds. These were several villages which were grouped together, the area usually being of a hundred hides (a hide was the area needed to support one peasant family). The hundred court dealt with private disputes as well as criminal cases, and all the inhabitants were expected to attend. The hundred in which Uxbridge was situated was known as Elthorne Hundred; it covered most of the area of the present London Borough of Hillingdon, stretching as far east as Brentford. The hundred remained an important unit of local government, half-way between the parish and the shire, until the nineteenth century when all its administrative functions were abolished.

We know little more of the early history of the Uxbridge area. All the evidence we have is from archaeology, the study of place-names (most of which, in this area, are of Saxon origin), and a few tantalising contemporary documents, such as the 'Anglo-Saxon Chronicle'. The first real picture we get of the Uxbridge area is in 1086, with the Domesday Book.

Finally, what happened to the people who were here before the Saxons? That is something we will never know, but some of them must have remained, for the river name 'Colne' is British, not Anglo-Saxon.

11

Chapter Two

Medieval Uxbridge

In the year 1066, as every schoolchild knows, William of Normandy defeated the Saxon army at the Battle of Hastings and assumed the sovereignty of England. He rewarded his followers by giving them the lands of the defeated Saxons. It was then necessary for him to know who owned what land, and how much it was worth. Accordingly, in 1086, he sent out his messengers to compile a list of all the landowners and the resources of England. This was the Domesday Book.

The landholding structure of eleventh century England was based on the manor rather than the village. Each village may have had more than one manor and at the same time a manor may have included more than one village. Therefore, if a particular village is not named in the Domesday Book it is often because it is included under another manor. Such is the case with Uxbridge. At the time of the Norman Conquest there were two manors which were concerned with the Uxbridge area. These manors were those of Colham and Hillingdon. Uxbridge was part of Colham manor. Some time in the fifteenth century the manors of Colham and Hillingdon were merged and the lands of the two are indistinguishable. No surveys were made of the manors before they merged so we cannot tell the exact area of each individual manor. Together the two manors covered most of Hillingdon parish. The Domesday Book provides us with a picture of these two manors as they were in 1086.

As both manors were relevant to the history of Uxbridge we shall look at both of them as they were. The area of Colham manor was twice that of Hillingdon, and obviously included lands along the Colne, for two and a half water mills are listed as belonging to the manor (we do not know who owned the other half mill; it is not listed among the possessions of any of the neighbouring manors). Hillingdon had no mills, but a weir, probably on the River Pinn, supplied the villagers with fish. Colham manor was also much better endowed with meadow land; it had enough to support twenty-four oxen, that is three plough teams, whereas Hillingdon had only enough to feed half a plough team, four oxen. The numbers of ploughs used on the manor were also listed in the Domesday Book. Hillingdon had four ploughs, two owned by the lord and two by the villagers. These were the greatest number of ploughs that the land could support. Colham, however, although it had enough land for seven ploughs, had only six in use, three by the lord and three by the villagers. This meant that not all the suitable land in the manor was cultivated. The most significant feature of the landscape of eleventh century Hillingdon was the amount of woodland. There was enough woodland to support over 1,000 pigs in Hillingdon alone. Colham has much less as most of its land was on the lighter soils near the river. Finally, there was a small vineyard in Colham manor. It has been said that Vine Street in Uxbridge was the site of this vineyard, from which it took its name, but this is only a legend with no truth in it; the street was known as Blind Lane until the nineteenth century.

Much less is known of the people who lived in the two manors. They were not listed by name, only by their status within the manor. The most important men were the villagers or villeins; ten of these lived in Colham and two in Hillingdon. Below them were the smallholders or bordars; of whom, again, ten lived in Colham and two in Hillingdon. The lowest in status of the freemen were the cottagers; of whom four lived in Colham and two in Hillingdon. Also working on the Colham estate were eight slaves. Hillingdon had two resident Frenchmen, probably Normans, with their own workers. Altogether forty-two men were listed, which indicates a population of around 200 in the whole area. There was a church to serve these people, as a priest is listed for Colham, although the church is assumed to be that at Hillingdon.

Thus the Uxbridge area gradually began to be developed. The rivers were harnessed to power mills; those woods which were not cleared for use as farmland were used to provide fodder for pigs. The population steadily increased, requiring an ever more complex social structure. The Norman Conquest did not alter the basic structure; rather it superimposed a foreign landlord at the head of it. It is unlikely that this change of landlords was of direct personal interest to the inhabitants of the Uxbridge area. Both Colham and Hillingdon manors had been owned by men who probably spent most of their time at the Court of King Edward the Confessor. Wigot of Wallingford, a close kinsman of the king, had held Colham. He was a great landowner, with estates in eleven counties, of which Colham was only a small manor. Ulf, who had held Hillingdon, was one of King Edward's military retainers. Both of these men were replaced by Roger de Montgomery, Earl of Shrewsbury, a cousin of William the Conqueror. He had large estates all over England and his Middlesex holdings covered most of the western boundary of the county. These estates became part of the Honor of Wallingford; their ownership passed through several hands until in 1179 they were in the possession of Gilbert Basset.

Basset's Grant

Although Uxbridge is only mentioned briefly before this date, that it existed is undeniable, although there is no archaeological evidence before the late twelfth century. Only a hundred years after Domesday Book was compiled the town of Uxbridge was granted its market charter. Basset's Grant is the first document to deal specifically with Uxbridge. It begins "Gilbert Basset to all Barons of the Honor of Wallingford, and his neighbours and friends, greeting. Know ye that our lord Henry, King of England, hath granted to me liberty to make a market in my town of Wxebruge." The market was to be held each Thursday and all profits arising from it were to belong to the lord. Any man who held either an acre or a half acre within the town was exempt from tolls on payment of an annual fine. By 1281 the town also had an annual fair held on St. Margaret's Day. The right to hold a second annual fair at Michaelmas and a Monday market was granted to the lord of Colham in 1294.

It can be imagined that from now on Uxbridge grew rapidly. Farmers and merchants from both Middlesex and Buckinghamshire would be attracted to this market, with its ideal position at a river crossing on the main road to Oxford. From those who came just once a week for the market some would have been induced to stay; and so gradually the small town grew, its houses straggling either side of the main street, with a few following the line of a side road to Windsor. As the population grew, the mother church at Hillingdon could not cope. About the year 1200 a chapel of ease was built in Uxbridge at the junction of the main street and the side road to Windsor, presumably in the market place. The chapel was dedicated to St. Margaret. As it was a chapel it had no burial ground; all the dead of Uxbridge were buried at Hillingdon, although all the church services could be held in the chapel.

This rapid increase in population and importance is reflected in the

St. Margaret's Chapel in 1809

fact that Uxbridge was one of only two Middlesex townships (the other was Brentford) to be represented at the first Parliament of Edward I in 1275. At some time before 1242 Uxbridge may have formed part of the Royal estates. This may explain some of the ambiguous aspects of the town's history. From 1293, and probably before, all the manorial courts for those manors in Middlesex belonging to the Honor of Wallingford were held in Uxbridge. This continued until the nineteenth century, when the courts were abolished. By the first quarter of the fourteenth century the population of the township of Uxbridge had outstripped the parent manor of Colham. In about 1335 a muster of men needed for military service required that Colham should contribute fifty-seven footmen and Uxbridge sixty-one men under three officers. This was one eighth of the total county force.

Despite the growing urban character of Uxbridge, the lives of most of its inhabitants were still firmly linked to agriculture. The tenants of Colham manor, including the inhabitants of Uxbridge, owed the lord of the manor various services as part of the conditions on which they held their land. These took the form of ploughing, harvesting etc. for so many days each year. By the beginning of the fourteenth century many people were paying money instead of performing the service themselves, and by the late 1380's money payments had entirely replaced labour services. This was a result of the great social upheavals caused by the Black Death after 1348, though we have no other evidence to show how it might have affected Uxbridge. At this period the demesne, that is the part of the manor owned and farmed by the lord, was divided into two parts. According to the Victoria County History of Middlesex "the northern estate was administered from a grange called Northall (somewhere in the area of the present Uxbridge Common). Each estate had a cowherd, swineherd and ploughman, and a warrener was appointed for the whole manor. In addition to the usual domestic and draught animals the stock included 60 cows, 100 pigs, and 400 sheep tended by a shepherd. Much of the demesne was in wheat; small quantities of rye and oats were grown. Of the total corn yield of 242 quarters in 1376, 105 qr. were sold, chiefly in London, 29 qr. sent to Uxbridge for malting and brewing, and 13 qr. milled for flour at Uxbridge and Colham."

The farming methods were those developed by the Saxons and were to continue until the nineteenth century. The system is known as open field farming. In this a farmer's holdings are divided into strips scattered amongst the strips of other farmers in very large fields. It is not known how many open fields there were around Uxbridge; however, they lay mostly to the south of the London-Oxford road and east of the River Frays. To the north and west were large areas of common and waste. The lord of Colham owned a rabbit warren on land that later became known as Uxbridge Common, and another in Hillingdon, at Coney Green (coney is another name for rabbit).

The road from London to Oxford and beyond was one of the major routes of medieval England. It is one of the five main roads marked out of London on the map known as the Gough Map of about 1360. Uxbridge is marked as the first stage on the journey from London. It seems that Uxbridge was always so recognised, for in 1314 the men employed to take horses to Oxford for the transport of the body of Piers Gaveston to Kings Langley spent a night in Uxbridge. The traffic on the road by this time would have been quite heavy, local farmers coming to market and people travelling longer distances. For all these people Uxbridge was the focus of their journey, at least for that day. The roads were not paved, so in wet weather would have been a quagmire of deep mud. Therefore, in 1358 Ellis Waleys of Uxbridge and two men from Acton were granted the right to pave sections of the road in Uxbridge, Acton and places in between.

Part of the importance of Uxbridge, as already stated, was as a crossing point on the River Colne. Although there is no indication of when the original bridge was built it was certainly before 1180, when it has become part of the place-name as written in Basset's Grant. A bridge is first mentioned in 1377, when a man named Gomme was ordered, as the owner of the ground on which the bridge stood, to repair it as it was described as being in a ruinous condition. According to Redford and Riches' 'History of Uxbridge' the bridge at this time was only adapted for foot and horse passengers; wheeled traffic had to use the adjacent ford. The bridge was in two distinct parts, divided by an island in the centre of the river.

The river provided the power for the mills which were another basis for the economic prosperity of Uxbridge. The two mills mentioned in Domesday Book are impossible to identify as throughout the Middle Ages the mills kept changing name and the evidence is very fragmentary. However, it is safe to say that throughout this period the number of mills along the Colne and Frays increased. The Frays is an artificial waterway which was constructed at this time in order to provide power for more mills. As late as 1419 the Colne was still navigable by small boats, which was taken advantage of by at least one mill, which had its own wharf on the river.

Uxbridge was continually expanding as both its population and its economy grew. From being a small settlement dependent on the weekly market it began to develop other trading and manufacturing interests in line with other medieval towns. Throughout its history, until recent times, the most important industries in Uxbridge were flour milling and brewing. The development of Uxbridge necessarily led to an increasingly complex social and economic organisation of the town. This was typified by the development of the guild. There was no trade guild in Uxbridge, (one in which membership was restricted to those following a particular craft). The guild of St. Mary and St. Margaret, founded in 1448, was a religious organisation for the social and spiritual benefit of the members. The guild protected the welfare of the members while they were alive and prayed for their souls after death. The officers of the guild would have been the wealthier and more prominent members of the community, although no records survive to show who they were. Despite the fact that the Uxbridge guild was not wealthy, its members were able to contribute enough money to rebuild completely part of St. Margaret's chapel. The entire south aisle was rebuilt and doubled in size to act as the guild's own chapel, for which it provided a chaplain and two chapelwardens. In 1548 the guild owned land in Cowley Field, the "George" Inn and shops and houses in Uxbridge, together worth £11. Also at this date, in 1446, Walter Shiryngton, Chancellor of the Duchy of Lancaster, applied for permission to found a chantry chapel. This was one in which a priest was employed perpetually to say prayers for the soul of the deceased. Shiryngton's chapel was built at the eastern end of the north aisle after 1459, the year of his death. The first priest was a man named Christopher Thole. Lands in Uxbridge, including the "Bull" and "Cross Keys" Inns, were provided to supply the income for the upkeep of the chapel. Both the guild and chantry chapels were dissolved in 1547, as part of the English Reformation, and their assets disposed of.

Economic prosperity was reflected in the appearance of the town. We have no idea of what Uxbridge looked like before the end of the fifteenth century, as, apart from the church, there are no buildings surviving from that date. We can assume, however, that the buildings were constructed of timber. The plots of land were long and narrow, so that as many people as possible could have a frontage onto the High Street. Traces of this can still be seen on a modern map of Uxbridge. Those people who lived in the Lynch (later Windsor Street) had much smaller plots of land as this area was developed later than the High Street. At this time the town would have comprised little more than the High Street and the Lynch, each lined with wooden buildings behind which would have been gardens and fields. Towards the end of the fifteenth century prosperous tradesmen and innkeepers began to rebuild their houses in a more modern fashion. Some of these buildings still survive. It you can imagine the High Street full of buildings such as the "Queen's Head" or the old "King's Arms", that is what Uxbridge looked like at the beginning of the sixteenth century. Most of these buildings were in timber, but a new material was just beginning to be employed. This was brick, and there are substantial deposits of brickearth around Cowley. One of the most important local buildings constructed in this new material was that now known as the "Crown and Treaty" Inn. This was built in the first half of the sixteenth century and was then known as Place House. It was then much larger, as the part that remains today is only one third of the original building. The main road did not then pass as close as it does today, but curved around the gardens to rejoin its present course at the High Bridge.

John Leland, the King's Antiquary, visited Uxbridge in the 1540's whilst on his travels, which were to result in the publication of his famous 'Itinerary'. His description of Uxbridge is as follows; "The whole town lieth from the west, rising a little to south-east. In it is but one long street: but that for timber is well builded. There is a celebrate market once a week, and a great fair once a year at the feast of St. Michael. There is a chapel of ease in the town. The parish church is almost a mile out of town, in the very highway to London, (called Great Hillingdon which is) a token that Uxbridge itself is no very old town.

There be two wood bridges at the west end of Uxbridge town, and under the westernest goeth the main arm of the Colne river. The lesser arm of the Colne goeth under the other (bridge) and each of them serves there a great mill."

By this time the town was rapidly taking up its position as the foremost market town of West Middlesex. A market house had already been built and the town's prosperity is reflected in the subsidies of the 1520's.

During the middle years of his reign Henry VIII was very short of cash, and between 1523 and 1527 he sought to remedy this by levying an annual subsidy on his subjects. This was levied on all those people worth one pound a year or more in either goods or wages. From this we can see the relative prosperity of Uxbridge as against other towns and the distribution of wealth within the town. Of the 153 people taxed in Hillingdon parish seventy-seven were from Uxbridge. The subsidy returns show how unequally the wealth was divided through the population. At the top, 5.2% of the taxpayers owned over 34% of the wealth, whereas 31% of the taxpayers owned only 5.6% of the wealth. This includes only those who were rich enough to be taxed; for there were many people who were too poor to pay any taxes at all. In other, similar towns, about a third of the population escaped tax. If this were true of Uxbridge it would make the total population of the town somewhere around 600, but this is only a very rough

The execution of John Denley

The Burning *of* M^R. JOHN DENLEY, *at* Uxbridge, *in* Middlesex.

estimate. Uxbridge was typical of most Tudor towns in that a small number of people owned most of the money and property in the town.

This economic prosperity led to increasing conflict within the town. Since Gilbert Basset had granted his charter the town had been run as part of the manor of Colham, and in turn as part of the Honor of Wallingford. The town had its own constables to enforce the rulings of the manor court. As the town grew more prosperous the people began to resent this outside control and to seek to overthrow it. Matters began to deteriorate in the early sixteenth century, when one of the Uxbridge constables was attacked and killed by the bailiff of Colham manor and his men. Discontent festered throughout the century and finally came to a head in 1630, when the dispute with the Countess of Derby, to be discussed later, resolved some of the more pressing grievances. The town continued to be governed by the honor court until it was abolished in 1813.

The mid-sixteenth century was a time of bitter religious controversy. In 1548 Edward VI dissolved the guild and chantry chapels, including those in Uxbridge. The break with the Roman Catholic Church grew more pronounced, since with Edward's accession England had officially become a Protestant country. Edward was succeeded by his sister Mary, who immediately returned the country to Roman Catholicism. Many people continued to support the Protestant faith, and Mary instituted a campaign of persecution against them. Three Protestants were burned at the stake in Uxbridge. They were not local men; their punishment was intended to set an example to the local people. The three men were John Denley, Patrick Packingham and Robert Smith. Denley, a gentleman from Kent, was arrested with a friend in Essex. He was tortured by the Bishop of London, Bishop Bonner, and refusing to recant his faith he was sentenced to be burned. Smith was a clerk in Holy Orders from Windsor. He too was sentenced to be burned at Uxbridge on the same day as Denley, the 8th August 1555. In Foxe's Book of Martyrs there is a vivid description of the death of Denley. "Being set in the fire with the burning flame about him, he sung in it a Psalm. Then cruel Doctor Story being there present, commanded one of the tormentors to hurl a Faggot at him, whereupon being hurt therewith upon the face that he bled again, he left his singing, and clapt both his hands on his face. Truly, quoth Dr. Story, to him that hurled the Faggot, thou hast mar'd a good old Song." The third man to die was Patrick Packingham, an itinerant workman, who was executed on the 28th of August the same year. The executions took place on the Lynch Green, which no longer exists. It was close to the site of the old burial ground, where there is now a memorial to the martyrs. Dr. Story was a leading anti-Protestant campaigner. He was executed at Tyburn for treason in 1571, when he was caught conspiring with the Spanish to restore England to the Roman Catholic Church.

The market house built at the beginning of the century must have been inadequate for the large market Uxbridge now enjoyed. In 1561 a new market house was erected at the eastern end of the site of the present market house. The new building was nearly square, being forty by forty-five feet. It took up nearly half the width of the High Street, leaving only twenty-one feet of roadway, while the entrance to the Lynch was reduced to only eight feet. Although we have these details we have no idea of what the building actually looked like. Even at this date the narrowness of the High Street at this point must have caused much inconvenience to travellers. Uxbridge continued to be the first recognised stage on the journey from London, and to meet the needs of the travellers a great many inns were built. This was commented on by William Camden in the 1580's, when he described Uxbridge as "full of inns."

This populous town was still only a chapelry of Hillingdon, without its own burial ground. As the population increased this must have become even more inconvenient. Therefore, in 1576 the Earl of Derby, then lord of the manor, gave a piece of land adjoining Lynch Green to be used as a burial ground. It was enclosed by a wall at the expense of Margery Legie, a widow. There is an inscription over the gateway to the ground commemorating this. For every person buried in the new ground the inhabitants of Uxbridge had to pay the Church at Hillingdon two pence, as the revenue from burials was a valuable part of church income.

A reconstruction of the former Market House by Mary Pearce

The increase in the prosperity of Uxbridge was not uniform. The almost total dependence on corn, for both the market and milling, made the town very vulnerable to any fluctuations in the harvest. When the harvest failed as it did in the years 1586-7 the town was described as being in "great distresse for want of corne". The Justices of the Peace of Hertfordshire and Buckinghamshire forbade the carrying of any corn to Uxbridge because of the scarcity in their own areas. They were requested by the Privy Council to allow farmers who normally took corn to Uxbridge to carry a proportion of their usual load to relieve the dearth in the town. Harvest failure was not the only thing to disrupt the market. In 1593 the annual fair was cancelled because of the outbreak of plague in the town. The reliance of the whole economy of Uxbridge on its corn market was to have serious repercussions later in its history.

The mid-sixteenth century in Uxbridge saw a large number of charities established. This implies two things; that there were people rich enough to endow the charities and also a large number of poor people to benefit from them. The oldest charity was that set up by William Skydmore, ironmonger of London but native of Uxbridge, in 1500. This provided twelve pence worth of bread to be distributed to the poor after divine service each Sunday at St. Margaret's. John Marsh's charity, of 1557, ordained that the Mercers' Company of London should furnish money to supply twenty-four poor people of Uxbridge with two shillings' worth of bread every Sunday. Robert Wolman left money from his Hillingdon, Cowley and London properties to maintain a school in Uxbridge. The school was never built. John Garrett, beer brewer of Uxbridge, left the income from various properties in Uxbridge, including shops and stalls in the market, to be paid by the Burgesses of Kingston-upon-Thames to the poor of Uxbridge. All of these charities were private attempts to alleviate the problems of poverty within the town.

The people of Uxbridge were no more peaceful nor more law-abiding than people elsewhere. The records of the Middlesex County Courts have many references to Uxbridge people being bound over to keep the peace or indicted for theft. Penalties were very severe; for example, in 1571 Lewis Jones of London stole some clothes and other goods from Hugh Nevill of Uxbridge worth nearly 26 shillings. He was sentenced to be hung. Fights could also get out of hand. In 1586 five Uxbridge men "were fighting together in the highway at Woxbridge with swords and staves"; John Bradley tried to stop them but was hit over the head and died instantly. The man who hit him, Robert Ingledon, was indicted for murder, but no sentence was recorded.

The sports with which the people of Uxbridge amused themselves have not changed much over the centuries. In March 1576 "at Ruyslippe co. Midd., Arthur Reynolds husbandman,... (etc)..., all of Ruyslippe aforesaid, Thomas Darcye of Woxbridge yoman, and William Davye taylor, Roger Okeley yoman, Thomas Harker husbandman, William Raynar husbandman, and Richard Parsonne husbandman, all seven of Woxbridge aforesaid, with unknown malefactors to the number of a hundred, assembled themselves unlawfully and played a certain unlawfull game, called footeball, by reason of which unlawfull game there rose amongst them a great affray, likely to result in homicides and serious accidents."

During the Middle Ages Uxbridge had grown from being a small market town, created as part of the perquisites of the Honor of Wallingford, into one of the most important marketing centres in Middlesex. The legacy of manorial control was to have its effect in the seventeenth century.

Chapter Three

The Seventeenth Century

During the early years of the seventeenth century, life in Uxbridge continued much as it had done formerly. The town continued to prosper as trade increased. The market, milling and inns remained the basis of the town's economy. In July 1602, Queen Elizabeth I visited the Countess of Derby at Harefield Place. Although it poured with rain throughout her visit, the people of Uxbridge would still have been excited by their Queen being so close. No doubt many of them lined the road to cheer as she passed through the town on her way to Harefield.

1603 was not such a happy year. In March the Queen died, which was a great shock to many of her people who had never known another sovereign. In the summer plague struck the town. 176 people died of the plague out of the 205 people buried in Uxbridge that year. Deaths on this scale must have seriously disrupted the life of the town. Whoever could afford it would leave the town and the sickness. The market, understandably, would lose its popularity. Travellers passing through would not want to stop in a plague-stricken town and the mills would run out of corn to grind if the market was closed. An outbreak of plague was both a personal and an economic tragedy for a town. The plague struck again in 1625, when 136 out of 162 burials were caused by the disease, and again in 1636. On the 3rd October, 1636, the Middlesex Sessions levied a rate on the county parishes to support those stricken with plague in the London area. Uxbridge was assessed at thirty shillings a week and Hillingdon at forty shillings. In the Great Plague of 1665 Uxbridge escaped fairly lightly; only half of the 81 deaths that year were caused by plague.

Despite these setbacks the economy of the town still prospered. As they grew richer and more numerous the townsfolk also became more militant, a reflection of the whole country at this time. The people of Uxbridge chose to dispute with the Lord of the Manor his (or her) right to the tolls from the market. Until 1637 the lordship of the Manor of Colham was held by the Countess of Derby, who lived at Harefield Place. (This house was adjacent to Harefield Church and was demolished in 1814.) It was her custom at the Manor Court, after formal acknowledgement of her right to the tolls, to hand all the money back to the bailiffs to expend on charitable purposes in the town.

In 1630 certain of the townsfolk, calling themselves burgesses although they had no legal right to the title, discovered Basset's Grant. They misread the document and thought that it said that they, rather than the Lord of the Manor, were entitled to the profits of the market. They regarded these tolls as their own perquisites and would have been unlikely to have used them for charitable purposes, as the Countess of Derby did. Indeed, they were later accused of misappropriating funds and spending the money on feasting themselves rather than the poor. At Easter 1630, at the Court Leet, held in a room over the Market House, the bailiffs and burgesses of Uxbridge refused to acknowledge the right of the Countess to the tolls. After much discussion her steward

Mural of Barbara Jones depicting the events of 1630-33

postponed the meeting until Whitsun. At the resumed meeting the steward arrived to find himself locked out of the Court Room. Although he tried to hold the meeting in one of the burgage tenements no decision could be obtained. The meeting was again adjourned until July, but there was still no settlement. The Countess by now was justifiably annoyed. On April 18th 1631 she sent an order to the bailiffs in which she said that although hitherto she had allowed them to collect and distribute the tolls, from henceforth she would arrange for their collection and distribution as she saw fit.

After the receipt of this order matters simmered for a few months, until July. At the Fair of St. Margaret, on July 20th., the Countess's steward arrived to collect the tolls from the cattle market. The toll was one penny each from the buyer and seller of each animal. The steward was preceded by a man named Humphrey Gilbert, an employee of a tanner named Edmund Baker. Gilbert persuaded the men in the cattle market that they were being overcharged, the Countess only being entitled to a penny a beast. This, though inconsistent with their claim that the Countess was not entitled to any of the tolls, was very popular with the traders in the market. The dispute continued the following day, and that night Baker, the ringleader, raised an armed mob. Next day, when the Countess's two stewards began to collect the toll-corn, Baker and his armed mob of about forty descended on the two toll-collectors, tore their clothes and threw them out of the market. Then Baker and his 'army', joined by the assembled townsfolk, forced the tradesmen to bring in their produce. At this point William Jarman, a constable, arrived. It was his duty to stop the unlawful assembly. Therefore, he stood in the market place calling out "Oyez! Oyez! Let no one presume to enter the Market House at his peril!" No one took any notice, and then Baker told Jarman to arrest one of the Countess's stewards. He did not know what to do. Then Sir Edward Carr, Justice of the Peace, arrived. He too tried to calm the situation, but Baker would have none of it. Baker even posted one of his own servants on the stairs up to the room over the Market House where the toll-corn was stored, armed with a drawn sword, a gun and a pistol loaded with hail shot.

Trouble broke out again on the market day of the following week. As the Countess's servant, Richard Lee, an elderly gentleman, was taking the toll-corn from the cart of a Mrs. Jeffreys he was attacked by Baker and several others, all armed. He was pulled out of his cart, almost losing his boot in the process, and severely bruised. Several hundred inhabitants then rioted and appropriated the toll-corn for themselves.

The Countess of Derby immediately started legal proceedings and writs were issued by the Crown. In Court the Uxbridge burgesses pleaded that they were only claiming their rights as laid down in Basset's Grant. The document was produced but neither the judge nor the burgesses' council could read the Latin. However, Mr. Moy, acting for the Countess, could do so, and he proved her right to the tolls. The Court decided in her favour, but the people of Uxbridge were not satisfied and the rioting continued. The Countess then commenced suit in the Court of Star Chamber, which effectively frightened the burgesses into submission. Twenty of them, with Edmund Baker at their head, humbly petitioned the Countess to stop the Star Chamber proceedings; they offered to submit entirely to her goodwill and not dispute the tolls with her any longer. However, once the case had come to Star Chamber it could not be stopped; the result was that Baker and the other burgesses were fined £220 — £20 for the King and £200 for Lady Derby. Baker and the others could not bear the consequences of their actions. They sent another grovelling letter to Lady Derby, begging her to let them off the fine. She did so, and the whole affair ended amicably with a feast held at the Court Leet on October 1st. 1633, with a gift of venison from Lady Derby. (A mural by Barbara Jones depicting scenes from these events can be seen in the foyer of the Civic Centre, Uxbridge.)

This action of the burgesses of Uxbridge, in rebelling against traditional authority, was not untypical of events in England at this time. The rumblings of discontent finally erupted into civil war in 1642.

The events leading up to the Civil War are much too complex to discuss here. Suffice it to say that when Charles I called the Parliament, later known as the Long Parliament, in October 1640, he was assembling his enemies together. The King needed money, which he could get only through Parliament; Parliament would not supply the money unless the King acceded to their demands. In 1641 Parliament drew up a manifesto, known as the Protestation, in which each member of Parliament swore to uphold the King, Parliament, the rights of individuals and the Protestant religion as expressed in the Church of England. Although this purported to be in defence of the King, Church and Constitution, it was in fact the exact opposite, attacking Charles and his friends.

As the King left London in January 1642 the obligation to sign the oath was extended to all males over the age of eighteen. The men of Uxbridge signed the oath in the church on February 23rd., 1642 in the presence of Thomas Twist, minister of St. Margaret's, the churchwardens and constables. Failure to sign incurred heavy penalties. 288 men signed the oath; none are listed as absent or refusing to sign. This is the first indication we have had for some time of the size of the population of Uxbridge, which is estimated at around 1,000 at this date. Although by modern standards this is not large, in the seventeenth century Uxbridge was regarded as a fairly populous small town. The population of the rest of the parish of Hillingdon was somewhere about 800, with 233 men signing the Protestation oath.

By the end of 1644 Charles I appeared to be losing the Civil War. He had lost the greater part of his soldiers and the whole of the North of England after the Battle of Marston Moor in July of that year. Cromwell was in the process of reorganising the New Model Army and in January, 1645, Archbishop Laud of Canterbury, one of the King's main supporters, was executed. Negotiations for a peace treaty began immediately after the Battle of Marston Moor, the initiative coming from Charles. Parliament decided to hold the discussions in the town of Uxbridge, which supported their cause, it being convenient for both sides. The treaty was an attempt by the Presbyterian party and the Scots to achieve their own ends; Cromwell and his Independents took no part. Thirty-two commissioners were appointed, sixteen for each side. Including all their assistants, servants and soldiers, and all the people who must have flocked to Uxbridge to see the great events taking place, the town must have been very full indeed for those few weeks in January and February 1645.

Edward Hyde, Earl of Clarendon, one of the King's Commissioners, has left a full description of those weeks in his "History of the Great Rebellion and Civil Wars", which Redford and Riches quote at length. The King's commissioners were given the whole of the south side of the High Street, with the exception of one house, for their accommodation. They took the Crown Inn for their headquarters. The Parliament men had the north side, with the George Inn as their headquarters. The atmosphere on each side of the street seems to have been markedly different, allowing for Clarendon's bias. The King's men, or Cavaliers, spent their time giving and receiving visits to and from all their friends and acting as though they were in their own homes. Among the Roundheads there was an atmosphere of gloom and mistrust. None of the Roundheads would allow himself to be seen alone with a Cavalier, but had always a companion, — often, as Clarendon says, a man he mistrusted.

The actual negotiations took place in the building now known as the "Crown and Treaty House" Inn. Clarendon says: "There was a good House at the end of the Town, which was provided for the Treaty, where was a fair room in the middle of the House, handsomely dressed up for the Commissioners to sit in; a large square Table being placed in the middle with Seats for the Commissioners, one side being sufficient for those of either party; and a Rail for others who should be thought necessary to be present, which went round. There were many other Rooms on either side of this Great Room, for the Commissioners on either side to retire to, when they thought fit to consult by themselves, and to return again to Publick Debate, and there being good Staires at either end of the House, they never went through each others Quarters, nor met but in the great Room." A room in the existing building has traditionally been known as that in which the treaty was discussed. This, however, is unlikely. The actual room was almost certainly in the central wing, demolished in the eighteenth century. The room remaining is more probably that to which the Commissioners retired. In 1924 the panelling from this room was sold to an American and installed in his office in the Empire State Building, New York. It was returned to England as a coronation gift for Queen Elizabeth II in 1953 and restored to the Inn, although the panelling still remains the property of the Queen. During the eighteenth century the main block and one side wing were demolished and the remaining building divided into several tenements. In 1785 improvements to the High Street meant that the line of the road was taken straight through the Treaty House gardens. Soon after this the building became an inn, with stabling for over over forty horses, which it has remained ever since.

The Treaty House in 1789

The day set for the opening of the treaty negotiations was also a market day. Traditionally a sermon was preached in St. Margaret's, and many of the visitors, townsfolk and market traders went to the church that day. The sermon was preached by Christopher Love, a staunch Puritan, then chaplain to the garrison at Windsor Castle. He told the people not to expect any good from the treaty, "for that they come from Oxford with their hearts full of blood, and that there was as great a distance between this Treaty and Peace as between Heaven and Hell." Love was clearly intending to stir up the people and cause a riot against the King's Commissioners. He was expelled from Uxbridge, but not otherwise punished for these seditious remarks. His career ended on the scaffold in 1651, when he was executed for High Treason while trying to restore the monarchy!

There was never any real expectation that the peace negotiations would achieve any result. After three weeks' discussion the Commissioners separated and returned to their respective headquarters. Uxbridge settled back once more into its usual way of life. The town had been garrisoned by Parliamentary troops since the hostilities began in 1642. They cannot have been very alert, for in April 1646 Charles I escaped from Oxford. He passed through Uxbridge to stop at the Red Lion, Hillingdon, where he stayed for several hours to rest and refresh himself before continuing his journey. In June, 1647, the Parliamentary Army, under the command of Oliver Cromwell, made its headquarters in Uxbridge, as the centre of a line stretching from Staines to Watford. Cromwell himself stayed at the Crown Inn, the former Cavalier headquarters, in 1645. The army was not being used to defend London but to threaten it. Parliament was trying to disband the army, with which Cromwell violently disagreed. So, on June the 2nd, he seized the King from the Parliamentary supporters who were holding him and moved his troops to the Middlesex border. This so frightened the men in Westminster that they acceded to his demands. At the end of June the army moved to Reading while negotiations were taking place in High Wycombe. It returned briefly at the end of July when on the way in to London. The garrison was finally removed in 1651.

After the execution of Charles I in 1649 life settled down again. The rule of Parliament and Cromwell was very strict. There was religious toleration, but only for Puritans; Anglicans, Roman Catholics and Quakers were all forbidden to worship. The Anglican minister of St. Margaret's was replaced by a Puritan. There were laws against drinking and many inns were closed. This would have hit the innkeepers of Uxbridge hard as there were over twenty inns in the town by 1648. The troubled times worried one man so much that he hid his savings in a wall at Fountains Mill. The coins were not rediscovered until 1895.

The very strict religious attitude of the times did not lead all people into a more Christian frame of mind. In October 1655 William Lovejoy, (a misnomer if ever there was one,) an edged-tool maker of Uxbridge, was prosecuted for the ill-treatment of his apprentice, Matthew Nicholas. Matthew's father complained that "the said William Lovejoy employed his said apprentice on the Lord's Day at severall tymes in goeinge for money due to the said master, sometymes two, three, four, fyve or sixe myles from home, in the gatheringe of wood and fewell upon the same day and that the said master did very much misuse his said apprentice by fasteninge of a lock with a chain to it, and tyinge and fetteringe him to the shoppe, and that the said master his wife and mother did most cruelly and inhumanely beat his said apprentice, and also whipp'd him until he was very blooddy and his flesh rawe over a great part of his body, and then salted him, and held him naked over the fyre, beinge so salted to add to his paine."

The Civil War and Commonwealth resurrected the old dispute concerning the market tolls. Alice, Countess of Derby, had died in 1637, aged 76. She was succeeded as Lord of the Manor of Colham by her grandson, Lord Chandos. As a Royalist sympathiser he left England in 1652. Never losing an opportunity, the townspeople of Uxbridge appropriated the tolls once more. After the Restoration Lord Chandos's successor filed a bill for restitution of the tolls. The result of this action is unknown, but he tried again in 1672, when the verdict was against the town. In 1669 the town of Uxbridge was separated from the manor of Colham and in 1695 the lordship of the new manor of Uxbridge was sold to seven Uxbridge inhabitants for the sum of £550. Thus the long-running dispute over the market tolls was finally settled. One of the inhabitants of

Uxbridge who bought the manor was an Edmund Baker, grandson of the man who fought the Countess of Derby. The other six men were John Dunstall, William James, Roger Brewer, Matthew Baker, Thomas Weiks and Edmund Blount.

After the Restoration of 1660 Charles II was perpetually short of money. The Civil War had been very expensive, both in money and men. One solution to this problem was the Hearth Tax which was imposed from 1662 until 1689. This was basically a tax of two shillings a year on each domestic hearth. Exemptions were made for those too poor to pay. In 1664 there were, in Uxbridge, 232 occupied houses eligible to pay tax compared with only 179 in the rest of Hillingdon. Nearly three-quarters of those houses had between one and four fire-places. There were few larger houses, although there were three with twenty hearths. One was certainly the Treaty House and the other two were inns. Analysis of these hearth tax returns compared with other towns shows that Uxbridge was among the more prosperous of the small market towns. Prosperous towns usually had a large number of poor people, attracted there by the prospect of work. Uxbridge, however, had a much lower percentage of these than might have been expected. This is probably because of the proximity of London, attracting the poor away from Uxbridge.

For the last quarter of the seventeenth century Uxbridge settled down once more to its accustomed prosperous life. The market continued to expand and the number of corn mills in the town increased; there were at least seven mills in Uxbridge by the turn of the century. The town also exploited its position on the Oxford Road by having, according to Richard Blome, "divers good and well accommodated inns and houses of entertainment" to attract travellers. The only major event to disturb the even tenor of life in the town occurred after the Glorious Revolution of 1688 when soldiers from the disbanded army of James II were in the Uxbridge area; "the Irish and Roman Catholics are in a great body about Uxbridge who burn, kill and destroy all they meet with', said one report to Lord Dartmouth. The market was unlikely to have been well attended at this time. The town was beginning to be overcrowded, to the extent that the west door of the church and windows in the south aisle were blocked up by shops built against the walls. Development began to extend beyond the town boundaries. The natural extension of the town was along the line of the High Street into Hillingdon parish. This was known as Hillingdon End, and although in spirit it was part of the town of Uxbridge it was treated administratively as part of Hillingdon. On the edge of town, sizeable houses, such as Belmont near Uxbridge Common, were erected.

One of the most significant factors in the lives of the people of Uxbridge was the development of non-conformist religious groups in the town. In the mid sixteenth century Queen Mary had felt it necessary to set the Protestant townspeople an example by executing three men on Lynch Green. This Protestant tradition remained strong in the town and was one of the reasons why Uxbridge was a Parliamentary stronghold during the Civil War. The Restoration of Charles II and the reintroduction of the Anglican Church would have been viewed with mixed feelings. The introduction of the set of acts known as the Clarendon Code, which enforced worship in the Church of England, affected the town directly. In 1662, Thomas Godboult, the Puritan minister of St. Margaret's, was ejected from his living for refusing to conform with the Code. There were at least two non-conformist sects worshipping in Uxbridge at this time. The Society of Friends, or Quakers, had met in the town since 1658. An early Quaker was William Winch, landlord of the George Inn and one of the leaders in the dispute with the Countess of Derby. The land on which the present Meeting House stands, then at the rear of the George Inn, was acquired in 1676 from William Winch. The first building was erected in 1692 and rebuilt in 1817; this is the present building. Quakers formed a small but very influential body in the commercial life of Uxbridge. Also founded in the late seventeenth century was the Old Meeting Congregational Church. In 1662 several ejected Puritan ministers gathered in Uxbridge. The most important was Hezekiah Woodward, ex-vicar of Bray and a former chaplain to Oliver Cromwell. Until his death in 1675 he led, in secret, a body of strict Independents (later known as Congregationalists) who met in private houses. Their Meeting House was built in 1716 and still stands.

During the seventeenth century, apart from a short time during the Commonwealth, the chapel of St. Margaret's did not have a permanent minister; rather it was administered by the Vicar of Hillingdon, who performed Divine Service at Uxbridge once a month, and that only in the morning. As the townspeople of Uxbridge had achieved their independence in so many ways, this remaining item of outside control was annoying. 'Townsend's Gift' gave Uxbridge some measure of ecclesiastical independence. Under the will of George Townsend, 1682, provision was made that the profits from certain properties in London should support a minister at the chapelries of Uxbridge and Colnbrook. Scholarships were also to be provided for students to attend Pembroke College, Oxford. Whenever a vacancy occurred at either Uxbridge or Colnbrook it was to be filled by one of these scholars. The minister was known as a Lecturer and his duties were to read prayers and preach on Sunday morning and to read prayers only in the afternoon. All other religious services were still performed by the Vicar of Hillingdon.

The people of seventeenth century Uxbridge were just as concerned with the problem of poverty as their ancestors had been. Several new charities were established in the seventeenth century, all very similar to those already described. One, however, is more interesting. That is Lord Ossulston's Gift. One day his lordship was driving through Uxbridge in his carriage when he ran over and killed a small boy. He felt so guilty that he set up a trust to enable poor children of Uxbridge to be apprenticed to handicraft trades. This was one of the more influential and useful charities operating in the town in the eighteenth and nineteenth centuries.

The seventeenth century was an important period in the history of Uxbridge. At no other time had national events impinged so closely on the lives of the inhabitants. Although the town outwardly appeared much the same at the end of the century, the mental attitude of the people had changed drastically from what it had been at the beginning. This century marks the change-over from the medieval world to the modern.

Chapter Four

The Eighteenth Century

Changes came slowly to eighteenth century Uxbridge. Throughout the century the most important factors in the economic development of the town continued to be the market, mills and inns. As the century progressed, national improvements in transport and agriculture increased their importance, particularly the market, until by the end of the century Uxbridge was the most considerable market town in Middlesex and a great area beyond. However, unlike many similar towns in the provinces, it did not develop as a social centre for the surrounding gentry; London was much too close. But the increased prosperity brought by trade gradually led to improvements in the town.

The first major improvement to benefit a large number of the inhabitants came in 1701. Mr. John Yarnold constructed a waterworks to supply water from the Colne to Uxbridge. Upon payment of one pound a year the water was laid on to individual houses. The water was supplied to the top of the town in the morning and the bottom in the afternoon one day and vice-versa the next. The pipes were made of wood; a fragment remains in the Hillingdon Borough Libraries Local History Collection. The waterworks were badly damaged during the digging of the Grand Junction Canal and the supply ceased in 1799. After this the town was without a regular supply of clean water until wells were dug at the behest of the Lords in Trust in 1800.

Although the Lecturer of St. Margaret's chapel had been assured of a reasonable income under the terms of George Townsend's will, he still did not have a permanent residence in the town. In 1705, therefore, the people of Uxbridge subscribed £126 to build him a house, with another £200 borrowed to complete the building. The house was erected in an acre of land bought from Cowley Field, behind Vine Street and extending to the Cowley Road. As one of the conditions of having the house, the Lecturer had to teach six poor boys of Uxbridge reading and writing. Girls were educated at the expense of the manorial trustees in premises which were part of the almshouses in the Lynch. A room over the Market House was also used as a schoolroom, probably for the boys. In 1728 the girls' schoolroom was rebuilt when the almshouses were redeveloped. From 1730 onwards part of the profits from the market were used to educate twenty boys and twenty-one girls from the town. They were taught reading, writing and arithmetic, and the girls were taught to sew. The classes were always well attended and freqently exceeded the numbers laid down.

This development was made possible by a change in the government of the town. In 1729 the surviving representatives of the five men who had bought the manor of Uxbridge in 1695 conveyed it to seven trustees, thereafter known as the Lords of the Manor in Trust, who were to use the manorial profits for charitable purposes in the town. The final Manor Court Leet, before it was abolished by the Lords in Trust, was held in 1727. This was an important meeting, for it led to a survey of the manor in which the boundaries of Uxbridge were defined for the first time. It is possible that it was at this time that the boundary was marked with a ditch, known as the Borough Ditch. Redford and Riches use the existence of the ditch to show that the town was an ancient borough. However, in the survey of 1727 the only ditches mentioned, apart from the Shire Ditch which marked the county boundary, are those occurring normally between fields. There is no evidence to prove this, but it is possible that the ditch which marked the northern boundary of the town was dug some time in the early eighteenth century. The boundary enclosed an area of eighty-five acres. The westernmost point was the High Bridge over the Colne, with Vine Street (then known as Blind or Woolwind Lane) forming the eastern boundary. The River Frays formed the southern boundary, while the northern boundary followed roughly the line of the modern York Road. This northern boundary was the most difficult to define as it ran across fields.

Eighteenth century Uxbridge was no better than any other town of the time. Despite the prosperity among certain members of the community there was still a great deal of poverty. The town was dirty and very smelly, the large number of inns encouraged drunkenness and the many travellers invited highwaymen. Looking back on past ages with rose-coloured spectacles is not the prerogative of our own times. In 1828 a correspondent to the *Uxbridge Note Book* felt impelled to correct a falsely Utopian picture of eighteenth century Uxbridge by giving his own account of the town in the early years of the century. A large part of his letter is worth quoting; *"Two or three facts were related to me by a Magistrate of a neighbouring county who died some years ago at a very advanced age, which, if correct, go far to prove exactly the reverse of some of Juvenal's* (the previous correspondent) *statements respecting our ancestors. Somewhat more than a century ago* (about 1720) *the high road through the Town was in so bad a state, and the nuisances and annoyances of all kinds so intolerable, that travellers were accustomed carefully to avoid passing through it, by crossing from Hillingdon to High Bridge over the waste lands on the north-east side of the Town. This speaks volumes against the boasted virtues, industry and absence of misery of our forebears. My informant recollected the Publicans' signs swinging from cross-beams over the street, the middle of which was a deep muddy kennel that received and retained the filth of the town, so that its poisonous miasma was plentifully conveyed to the lungs of the inhabitants.*

"When Sir John Fielding presided over the police of the metropolis, the number and turpitude of the criminals brought before him from the Lynch (now Windsor Street) *induced him to call it Hell. This street was at that time notoriously the haunt of Thieves, Pickpockets etc. who exercised their callings in open day; and no-one thought of encountering the risk of passing through it by night.*

"There are still old inhabitants who recollect Hawke (William Hawke, 1750-74) *and other notorious Highwaymen living there publicly, and, under pretence that they would never rob an Uxbridge man, and giving it out as their determination that they would never be taken alive, they defied the law with impunity.*

"Even down to the period when Juvenal tells us 'joy and gladness beamed in every countenance' the generality of tradesmen in other points respectable, indulged habitually in gluttony and drunkenness. They sallied forth at midnight, pulled down their neighbours' shutters — broke their windows and even into their houses — painted the White Horse black etc.. Their feasting began in the morning — the sole business of their lives appeared to be eating and drinking — and

indulging in practical jokes without counting the cost. Woe to Juvenal's Vines and Fig-trees — he never heard of the "Marlow Men" ".

"*Q. 1st April 1828*".

The *Uxbridge Note Book* was a little magazine published monthly for one year in 1828 by Thomas Lake. Its sole aim was to reveal any incompetence in the administration of the town and to describe some of its evils so as to initiate reforms. Most of the contributions were in the form of letters, as the one above, all signed with pseudonyms. The 'Marlow Men' referred to at the end of Q's letter were Uxbridge's own version of the notorious Mohocks of eighteenth century London.

The food and drink trades were a very important part of the Uxbridge economy. In the eighteenth century, well over a quarter, and probably much more, of the population of the town were employed in supplying food and drink. By 1750 there were over forty licensed alehouses in the town and two breweries. Harman's brewery was founded in about 1729 and continued to brew beer until 1964. Norton's brewery was founded in 1750, on the north side of the High Street. Later in the century the Norton family expanded into other areas of business, particularly banking, and their interest in brewing had ceased by the 1830's. The inns were not only places for food and drink; they formed a vital part of nearly all aspects of eighteenth century life. There were four major inns in Uxbridge: the Crown, the George, the White Horse and the King's Arms. These were the largest and wealthiest as well as the oldest of the Uxbridge inns. They were posting inns, providing a meal and a change of horses for travellers, as well as overnight accommodation. Fifteen miles was about the furthest distance a team of horses could travel at any speed while pulling a coach. Uxbridge was ideally placed to change horses, being fifteen miles from Tyburn (now Marble Arch) and the same distance from High Wycombe, the next major stopping point on the Oxford Road.

Hillingdon Turnpike c.1840

The amount of traffic using the Uxbridge Road was greatly increased when the roads were improved with the introduction of Turnpikes. Until this time the responsibility of repairing any road fell on the parish through which it passed. This was particularly hard on those parishes which had a heavily used road, and consequently repairs were often done badly or not at all. With a Turnpike Act a Board of Trustees took over a length of road, became responsible for its maintenance and in return could charge tolls for the use of the road. In order to collect the tolls, gates were set up at intervals along the road, and it was these which gave the system its name; they were known as turnpikes. The first act for repairing and improving the road between Tyburn and Uxbridge was passed in 1714. This Act cost the Trustees £162. 11. 6, with expenses ranging from £55 for the fee for the Bill to be passed to the House of Lords to sixpence to a man to take the Act to the printers. There were sixty-nine trustees named, many of whom were local gentry, such as the Pagets of West Drayton, the Newdigates of Harefield and Sir Robert Vyner of Ickenham, as well as some of the more prosperous local tradesmen. The tolls to be collected were set out in the Act. They were:

6d. coach, chaise, chariot or calesh drawn by 6 horses
4d. coach, chaise, chariot or calesh drawn by 3 or 4 horses
2d. coach, chaise, chariot or calesh drawn by 2 horses
1d. calesh or chaise drawn by 1 horse
2d. waggon, cart or carriage drawn by 1 horse
3d. waggon, cart or carriage drawn by 2 or more horses
1d. horse, mule or ass, laden or unladen (and not drawing)
10d. per score every drove of oxen or neat cattle
5d. per score every drove of calves, hogs, sheep or lambs

The only horses exempt from toll were those carrying the mail, a horse ridden by the owner of a carriage passing at the same time, and those carrying people to vote in an election. This act was amended in 1726, 1741, 1776, 1793, 1801 and 1812, when on each occasion the number of trustees and the tolls to be charged were increased. The turnpike gates for Uxbridge were outside each end of the town, where the jurisdiction of two different trusts ended. The Tyburn to Uxbridge Trust gate was near the top of the Greenway, at what is now called Turnpike Lane. The Aylesbury and Wendover Trust gate was in Denham. Despite the number of acts passed to ensure the correct maintenance of the road it continued in a very bad state. Writing in 1798, in his '*View of the Agriculture of Middlesex*', John Middleton states: "The road from Tyburn through Uxbridge is supposed to have more broad-wheeled waggons pass over it than any other road in the country. Therefore, if broad wheels were advantageous to the roads, this would be in high condition, as it certainly is sufficiently rolled; and it has also the advantage of lying on a bed of gravel. But these, and the present management, are insufficient to keep it in repair.

"During the whole of the winter of 1797-8, there was but one passable track on this road, and that was less than six feet wide, and was eight inches deep in fluid mud. All the rest of the road was from a foot to eighteen inches deep in adhesive mud.

"This track was thronged with waggons (many of them drawn by ten horses and having broad wheels, even to sixteen inches wide) and farmers'

Uxbridge Market House, from Redford and Riches: 'History of Uxbridge', 1818

six-inch wheel carts, which occupied almost the whole of this confined space. It was therefore with great difficulty, and some danger, that horsemen and light carriages could pass.

"The road continued in this infamous condition during the whole winter half-year. No exertions were made towards cleansing it, although an expenditure of such a trifle as twenty-pounds, in the employment of a road-scraper drawn by one horse, would have effectively kept it clean and dry; and would also have prevented the destruction of upwards of three hundred pounds' worth of materials, that were reduced to mud by being soaked and ground, for six months, in water mixed with pounded flints.

"The only labourers to be seen on the road, during several succeeding months, were those of a neighbouring gentleman; and they were employed in carting the footpath into his enclosures.

"The tolls taken at the gates amount to a very large sum annually; and, as nothing is done towards keeping the road in repair, an enquiry ought to be instituted, as to what becomes of the money so collected.

"I do not mean, in the smallest degree, to insinuate that any of the trustees apply the principal to their own use, but the public have a right to expect that the tolls should be let for the greatest possible sum, and that the money so raised should be laid out in such a manner as to render the road clean and comfortable".

Despite Middleton's comments the turnpikes did improve travel between Uxbridge and London. By the 1780's it took just two hours to travel between the two towns. However, while travel on the open road was improved, delays were still caused in Uxbridge. The Old Market House had reduced the width of the High Street to only twenty-one feet. This was only just enough room for two carriages to pass, and on market days even this was impossible. At the west end of the High Street the road between the bridge over the Frays and the High Bridge was very narrow and circuitous as it passed round the outskirts of the grounds of the Treaty House. The High Bridge was rebuilt in 1768 as a seven-arch brick bridge. In 1785 an Act of Parliament was obtained to allow the Old Market House to be demolished and the road straightened. At the same time the opportunity was taken to pave and light some of the main footpaths in the town. The provisions for this were extended in 1806. According to Redford and Riches "the improvements made in the town, by the provisions of this act, were numerous and very considerable; so much so, as to give it quite a new aspect and make it assume to strangers, the appearance of being built in modern times".

The new Market House was the most striking building in late eighteenth century Uxbridge. It symbolised the supreme importance of the corn trade to this small town. By the 1780's the sixteenth century building had become totally inadequate for the amount of business transacted, apart from causing traffic bottlenecks in the High Street. Not only was the old Market House demolished but also a line of cottages fronting the High Street between the Market House and the entrance to Windsor Street. The first stone of the new building was laid on May 28, 1788, by Mr. Edward Payne, to the accompaniment of the church bells. The new building was designed by Mr. Thomas Neill and built by Messrs. Busby, Best and Powell. It was completed within the year and cost nearly three thousand pounds. The cost was met partly through voluntary subscriptions and partly from a loan from the Lords in Trust, which was soon paid off by the increased revenue from the market tolls. (The new building was the property of the Lords in Trust until 1981, when it was sold to an insurance company.) The new building covered the whole area between the two entrances to Windsor Street, the church and the High Street. The High Street frontage, which was now in line with the rest of the buildings in the street, was 140 feet long. The rooms above the Market House were designed to store corn, but they were soon used for many other functions. Both the Boys' Free School and the Girls' School of Industry were housed there, as were such social activities as the Reading Society, the Auxiliary Bible Society and the Savings Bank.

The problem of poverty in eighteenth century Uxbridge did not decrease as the century wore on. It is estimated that well over one third of the population were truly poor. However, methods were devised to deal with this problem as well as was possible according to the attitudes of the time. The poor were divided into two classes, the deserving and the undeserving. The deserving poor were those who were unable to support themselves through no fault of their own; through sickness, old age or extreme youth. For these people charity included money, food, nursing, clothing and even burial. The rest of the poor, — the "undeserving poor" — either received no relief or they had to earn it performing tasks in the workhouse. These tasks were usually breaking stones for road mending or picking old rope to pieces. The money to finance the poor relief came from rates levied on every householder. In Uxbridge it was administered by two Overseers of the Poor, elected annually. The Overseers usually came from the upper level of town society; they were generally prosperous tradesmen. They, and the rest of the ratepayers, had a vested interest in ensuring that expenditure remained as low as possible. The only people entitled to receive poor relief in Uxbridge were those who were either born here or had lived here for some time. Pregnant pauper women, travelling on the road, were quickly hustled into the next parish to ensure that when the child was born it was not a charge on the people of Uxbridge. This explains the constant references in the Overseers' accounts to payments to 'big-bellied' women. This also applied to every other parish in the country.

The system of providing for the deserving poor was divided into two parts, usually called 'Indoor' and 'Outdoor' relief. Those too old, too young or too sick to take care of themselves were taken into the workhouse, which had been built in 1728 on Lynch Green. The workhouse was not a pleasant place. A correspondent to the *Uxbridge Note Book* wrote; "Being 'brought to the workhouse' was, in days past, an evil too dreadful to be comtemplated. The possibility of such an event drove the sluggard from his bed, the drunkard from his pot and the sensualist from his low pleasures. To keep an aged parent from the parish was the pride and glory of children, and the dread of parochial relief to the child, embittered the passing moments of the dying parent''. Throughout the eighteenth century the management of the workhouse was contracted out; that is, someone agreed, for a fixed sum each year, to run the workhouse. There are no records remaining to show how the workhouse was run, but the system was harsh and open to corruption. Most of the contractors endeavoured to make as much profit as possible for themselves, while spending as little as possible on the paupers in their charge. The 'Outdoor' relief was administered directly by the Overseers and all their payments were noted in their account books. The payments made during the week of the 15th February, 1750, are a very good example of the way in which the poor on 'Outdoor' relief were catered for at this time:

	£	s	d
Clothing for Ann Man to Service (as a servant)	1	6	0
Thos. Reden for Straw & Thatching & Hurdle stuffs	0	9	0
Gave Fox	0	5	0
Gave Mr. Glover's man as was	0	3	0
Paid for a woman nursing Copeland's family	0	10	0
Laying out Old Roe	0	0	6
Two woollen shrouds	0	0	7
4 men carrying him to be buried	0	2	0
2 affidavits	0	2	0
Gave a poor man	0	0	6
John Howse & Thos. Copeland	0	4	6
Widow Hardman & Thos. Fletcher	0	4	6
Widow Kibbs & Bowell	0	1	6
Widow Cox & Elizabeth Ray	0	1	6
Widow Porton & Thos. Copeland	0	2	0
Francis North & Myfoot for the children	0	2	6
Sarah Reeves	0	1	0
Gave a sick man & woman	0	2	0
Gave a sick woman & 2 children	0	0	6
	3	16	7

Payments such as these enabled the poor to go on living in their own homes, but it was always seen as a last resort, while the workhouse was to be avoided if at all possible. In 1775 the workhouse contained sixty inmates, and the poor rate yielded £410. Relief provided from the poor rate was augmented by the various charities already mentioned and also by the Lords in Trust, who spent an increasing amount of the manorial profits on poor relief. In 1748 the Lords spent £58 on occasional relief to ninety-five townspeople, twelve non-townspeople and sixteen tenants of the almshouses. By 1778 almost two-thirds of the manorial profits of £378 were spent on the poor. Despite the ever increasing payments the problem of poverty in Uxbridge was never quite so acute as in similar towns elsewhere, as the proximity of London usually served to draw off some people.

Although lacking the fervour of the seventeenth century, the non-conformist religious sects in Uxbridge were still active. Of all the sects, the Quakers suffered most from loss of interest. By 1724 the meetings were poorly attended and the group was in debt. The Meeting House was so neglected that it had to be rebuilt in 1755. Interest revived, however, towards the end of the century when the Hulls and other wealthy Quaker families settled in Uxbridge. They were rich corn-millers, related to other prominent Quakers and friends of such people as Elizabeth Fry, the reformer, who visited them in Uxbridge.

John Wesley, who preached in Hillingdon and Uxbridge in 1754 and 1758, was the inspiration of the evangelical revival that swept through the Church of England in the latter part of the eighteenth century. This movement prompted a group of Anglicans to commence their own religious meetings in a room at the George Inn in 1770. By 1796 a meeting house had been built in the Lynch. It was erected in the garden of his house at his own expense by Job Arnold Glover, a merchant grocer. The chapel, later known as Providence Congregational Church, had its own burial ground and soon became one of the most influential forces in Uxbridge, for many of the town's important citizens were members of the congregation. In 1812 the Rev. George Redford was instituted as minister; he was one of the co-authors, in 1818 of the *'History of the ancient town and borough of Uxbridge'*.

His fellow writer, Thomas Hurry Riches, solicitor and banker, was a member of the Old Meeting House congregation, which had not suffered by these new developments. From 1769 until 1789 the minister was the Rev. Dr. William Rutherford, an eminent scholar. He opened a school in his house on Uxbridge Common. This was developed by his successor, the Rev. Dr. Thomas Ebenezer Beasley, and eventually moved to premises in Old Meeting House Yard, later known as Beasley's Yard. This school, which was known as the Uxbridge School, had a very good reputation and lasted until 1880. Throughout the eighteenth century non-conformists and dissenters were barred from sending their sons to the established public schools and universities. Such establishments as the Uxbridge School filled the gap, and often provided a much better education, as they were not afraid to experiment and had to produce good results in order to stay in business. Neither were the local children neglected, for a Sunday School, the first in the town, was set up at the Old Meeting House by 1792.

During the eighteenth century the Church of England was not particularly active in religious arguments; most developments were concerned with the church fabric rather than doctrine. St. Margaret's was typical of its period. The first major expenditure was in 1716 when a gallery was built at the west end of the chapel. In 1717 the bells were replaced. This was a costly and time-consuming business, as the chapelwardens' accounts for replacing the tenor bell shows;

	£	s	d
Charges in taking down the tenor	0	5	0
Charges in loading the tenor	0	1	0
Richard Smith for carrying the tenor to Cranford	0	2	6
Saml. Swift for carrying the tenor by water to London	0	1	6
The carriage for the tenor from London	0	16	0
For a horse to go to the bell-hangers	0	1	0
For a wheel for the saints bell	0	9	0
	1	16	0

The cost was met partly through the church rates and partly from donations. The bells were an important part of eighteenth century life. They were rung not only for the church services but also whenever there was any important news. In an age when few people had their own clocks, the church bells acted as an alarm when they rang each morning at five o'clock; and each evening the curfew rang at eight. The interior of the chapel was not neglected; in 1734 it was 'ceiled and beautified', and further alterations were made in 1771. Other projects which the Church Vestry were involved in included the building of a small lock-up cage for prisoners awaiting trial. This was built behind the new Market House in 1788. A fire-engine was purchased in 1770, with its own house on Lynch Green. The expense was met partly out of the church rates, partly by private subscription, and the Sun Fire Insurance Company gave twenty pounds towards it. According to Redford and Riches it was only used once, in 1796, when Mercer's Mill burnt down. As the population of the town increased in the eighteenth century, the burial ground became inadequate. In both 1782 and 1789 the ground was enlarged and the encircling wall rebuilt.

By the middle of the eighteenth century Uxbridge had developed into a small social centre. It never grew into the sort of fashionable social capital that other provincial towns did, as London was too near. However, for the local tradesmen and others for whom London was too expensive, Uxbridge was ideal. The social life was not hectic; rather it seems to have consisted mainly of dining, supping and drinking tea in different houses, interspersed with gentle walks in the garden or up and down the High Street. In many respects Uxbridge was very similar to the little town of Highbury in Jane Austen's *'Emma'*. We have a very good picture of life in the town in the 1780's from a series of letters written by James Scott to his daughter, Anna Maria Norton, known as Nancy. She was the wife of Daniel Norton, the miller, brewer and banker, and was staying at Malvern Wells, Gloucestershire, to recover her health, possibly after the birth of one of her ten children. While she was away her father wrote her long letters in the form of a journal; those we have cover the period July 17th to August 6th, 1780, when she returned to Uxbridge. An extract from one of these letters gives a very good impression of the sort of life lived by the more wealthy Uxbridge people and the subjects that concerned them:

"July 21st., 1780. I was so lame[1] last night I could not go to Thurbins. Took a walk in Mr. Aldridge's garden then supt at Aunts with Mrs. Howard. Mr. Rutherford[2] called and could hear no tidings of Billy but a Gentleman has promised him when the Bombay Ships come in that he will make all the enquiry possible and write him word. Mr. Rutherford's arm is in a sling but is better. We have had the Devil in Uxbridge a few nights ago as related by one Bob Redman who was a most swearing

wicked fellow. On his going down the Lynch he saw a man in black he thought was one of his acquaintances, but coming up to him he seized him by the collar and with an irresistable force dragged him to the Moor where he hauled him about over hedge and ditch and through the river until morning. Believe it was a blundering Devil that did not understand his business, for poor Bob has not swore an oath since and will make an excellent acquisition to the sanctified flock in George Yard.[3]
3 was hanged yesterday and 5 will be hanged today.[4] There has been a desperate engagement[5] between the Prudentia *and Captn. Waldegrave of 36 guns and the* Capricieux *a large French frigate (the contest was two hours) which we took having killed them 50 and 50 wounded and disabled the ship so much that we hardly had time to save the rest before she sunk. Her two Captains are killed. The* Prudentia *had 19 killed and 21 wounded.*
Mr.[6] dines out today so I shall dine at Aunts. Fancy I shall go today or tomorrow to Mr. Wilds and it's possible I shall have no more to say to you so conclude with my blessing to you and Becky. Kind respects to Mrs. Mary.

I am, dear Nancy, your sincere affectionate father
James Scott".

The Robert Redman mentioned in the letter was a famous Uxbridge character. This is a description of him written in 1824, near the end of his life: 'This noted character is a native of Uxbridge, in Middlesex, was born in a house on Tattle Hill in that town, and for many years was a bricklayer. He was a man of great strength and foremost in every dangerous enterprise. He was not content with the homely food of his fellow workmen but would indulge himself, now and then, with a kitten, cat or rat, which to his palate was 'most delicious'. He had so frequently eaten the dram glass after he had swallowed the gin that a late worthy landlady of the Chequers Inn would not allow him one, but gave him the liquor in a pewter measure. Half-pence, penny pieces, half-crowns and red hot tobacco pipes he has swallowed in abundance. He once challenged a famous jumper, Bob stipulated that he would choose his own ground and strange to tell he took the poor fellow to the top of the Church Steeple, stripped himself and jumped into the reservoir below with seven feet of water in it, which at that time supplied the town, and desired his adversary to follow him, but he declined and lost his Guinea, Bob having made the agreement for each to make one jump only. He has pinned a bull more than once like a mastiff and once rode an unruly bull from Cranford to Hatton, where the poor animal laid down with him through fatigue....He has always been a very fierce fellow, yet he is believed to have been strictly honest. He is now in the Workhouse at Uxbridge, is in good health, and was 90 years old last Michaelmas".

Social activities in Uxbridge were not always so bizarre as those enjoyed by Robert Redman. One of the most enduring, and for many people the most popular, was cricket. The game is first mentioned as being played on Uxbridge Moor in 1735. Thus Uxbridge is the oldest cricket club in Middlesex. Throughout the century games were played on Uxbridge Moor, including such matches as England v Kent, which England won by an innings and ten runs, in 1789. The club continued strong throughout the nineteenth century and it is still flourishing. By the 1820's the club had moved to Uxbridge Common and in 1858

---

1. Mr. Scott had gout. 2. The minister of the Old Meeting House. 3. Providence congregation. 4. Results of the Gordon Riots, June 1780. 5. The American War of Independence. 6. Mr. Daniel Norton.

moved again to its new ground in the centre of Uxbridge. This became known as Cricketfield Road and was the home of the club until 1971, when the development of the Civic Centre forced its removal to Park Road. One famous club member, from 1902 until 1914, was Bernard Bosanquet, who invented the googly. In the early days gambling on the result was at least as important as the match itself, if not more so. Prize fighting was also an extremely popular, if illegal, sport. In 1791 there was an attempt to stage a fight between the champion, Mendoza, and Ward on the Cricket Ground, Uxbridge Moor, but this was frustrated by the vigilance of the magistrates.

In 1797 the Uxbridge Yeomanry Cavalry was formed as a troop of volunteer cavalry in response to the threatened invasion of England by the French Revolutionary Army under Napoleon. As each man had to supply his own horse and equipment, only the wealthier members of the community were able to participate. They were not only afraid of invasion but also of revolution by the poorer members of English society. The Uxbridge Yeomanry were commanded by Sir Christopher Baynes of Harefield Place, with Gregory Way, younger son of Benjamin Way of Denham Place, as Lieutenant and Thomas Osborne of Uxbridge, timber merchant, as Cornet. The troop trained and exercised on Uxbridge Moor, but were disbanded in 1801 after the fears of invasion and revolution had died down.

During the second half of the eighteenth century Uxbridge began to expand commercially. The market remained the most important factor in the economy of the town. In 1784, at the time when the Market House was being rebuilt, the number of cattle fairs was increased to four a year; that is, on 25th March, 31st July, 29th September and 11th October. In common with other towns elsewhere, service industries developed to meet the needs of the inhabitants. One such was Thomas Lake's printing press, set up in 1770. Most of the remaining examples of the work of this firm date from the nineteenth century and include such items as sale catalogues, Redford and Riches' *'History of Uxbridge'* and the Uxbridge directory until 1853. In 1828 Lake's published the *'Uxbridge Note Book'*, a series of pamphlets attacking the local administration.

The growing economic complexity and increasing wealth of Uxbridge made the traditional simple financial arrangements inadequate. Therefore, in 1791, two cousins, Norton and Mercer, founded the Uxbridge Bank. It is not entirely clear which two members of these families were involved with the bank. Both the Nortons and the Mercers were rich brewing and milling families whose various members played an important part in the economic development of Uxbridge. It is probable that Norton was Daniel, husband of Nancy whose father wrote such long letters. The bank was set up in premises at the west end of the High Street, now known as Old Bank House. Daniel Norton died in 1794, after which the Bank was owned by the brothers John and Nicholas Mercer. John Mercer was probably the other original founding partner. The Mercer brothers were declared bankrupt in 1805, after which the Bank was acquired by John Hull. A new bank opened in 1806, trading as Hull, Smith and Norton, later Hull, Smith and Co. Despite various changes in the partnership, particularly in the early nineteenth century, the Bank remained firmly in the control of Uxbridge men until 1900, when it was amalgamated with Barclays Bank.

Facing: Robert Redman

The most important economic and industrial development in eighteenth century Uxbridge was the opening, on the 3rd of November, 1794, of the Grand Junction Canal. The Act of Parliament needed to build the canal had been passed in 1793 and digging had begun almost immediately on Uxbridge Moor. The section from the Thames to Uxbridge was finished by 1794 and was opened with a grand waterborne procession from Brentford to Uxbridge. In his history of the Grand Junction Canal, Alan Faulkner, quoting the *Northampton Mercury*, describes the events thus: "The opening of this part of the Canal was celebrated by a variety of mercantile persons of Brentford, Uxbridge, Rickmansworth and their vicinities, forming a large party, attended by a band of music, with flags and streamers, and several pieces of cannon, in a pleasure boat belonging to the Corporation of the City of London, preceding several barges laden with Timber, Coals and other Merchandize to Uxbridge". Much work remained to be done and it was not until 1800 that the canal provided a through route to Birmingham.

The canal stimulated industry, particularly the market, and several wharves and warehouses were built alongside the canal. By 1799 almost 10,000 tons of corn were carried between the Thames and Uxbridge each year, nearly all of which was milled in the town. According to Redford and Riches there were three corn mills in the town, and ten more within four miles, all along the rivers Colne and Frays, which were capable of supplying 3,000 sacks of flour a week.

The Uxbridge Panorama showing part of the north side of the High Street with the Bell and Sun Inns

As the centre of such an important agricultural area, much local industry was designed to satisfy the special needs of farmers. Markets and fairs brought so many people into the town that the High Street was soon well supplied with shops, selling all the necessities and many of the luxuries of life.

At the end of the eighteenth century Uxbridge was at its most prosperous. The population was rapidly increasing. In 1782 there were 1,212 people and by 1801 this had almost doubled to 2,000, although the number of houses had only increased from 366 to 395. Thus the town was beginning to be dangerously overcrowded. Its prosperity was amply evidenced by its outward appearance. The town which saw the close of the eighteenth century did not look at all the same as that which had seen its beginning. Few of the old timber-framed buildings remained; they had either been rebuilt or refronted so as to appear new. A very good example of this is 119 High Street, at present a restaurant (and originally the Falcon Inn, which later removed next door). This has an eighteenth century brick front on the sixteenth century timber frame. At some time around 1800 William Burgiss painted the "Uxbridge Panorama" on two long narrow strips of paper pasted on linen, showing every house on both sides of the High Street, which justifies Redford and Riches' description of the town as having "the appearance of being built in modern times". This was the affluent face of Uxbridge. The hovels of the poor were hidden away down alleys behind the High Street. As the population grew, the pressure on these yards became intense, but it was in the nineteenth century that the problem was to become most acute.

Chapter Five

The Nineteenth Century

The nineteenth century was a period of profound change for Uxbridge. Until this time all developments in the town had been centred on the market. The coming of the railways changed this, and by the end of the century Uxbridge market, which had been one of the largest in the country, was almost non-existent. This had far-reaching effects on all other aspects of the town's economic and social life. Early nineteenth century developments were concerned mostly with social and educational ideas. In 1836 the supremacy of Uxbridge in the district was acknowledged with the creation of the Uxbridge Poor Law Union, but in 1838 the town was by-passed by the Great Western Railway, whose station was at West Drayton. Much traffic immediately disappeared from the roads, and town and market went into a decline. After this date new industries, depending on the railways, were developed in the town. The market and inns lost much of their business and by the end of the century several of the inns had either been demolished or converted to other uses. This was also partly a result of the changing Victorian attitude to drink. The decline of the market meant that by the end of the century Uxbridge had become merely the shopping centre for a small local district.

These changes are reflected in the population changes in Uxbridge. In 1801 there were 2,111 people living within the town boundaries. This number rapidly increased until in 1841 there were 3,219. However, it was at this date that the town started to decline and the population remained stable, until by 1901 there were 3,063 inhabitants. The number of houses to accommodate these people rose from 385 in 1801 to 574 in 1831. Many of these new houses were slums, quickly erected by speculative builders in the yards, alleys and gardens behind the High Street. By the middle of the century almost every spare plot of land within the town boundary was built on. These dwellings were insanitary and overcrowded. Most of the better class housing was built outside the town, particularly along the London Road, near the entrance to Hillingdon House, after the fields of Hillingdon parish were enclosed in 1812. In the 1850's the presence of the Royal Elthorne Light Militia led to the development of the Greenway area, with substantial homes for the officers.

The speculative building already mentioned caused much contemporary disquiet. In the *'Uxbridge Note Book'* of 1828 the increase in crime and destitution was said to be caused by the rapid growth in the number of cottages. "Instead of the poor being domiciled in the neighbouring country where free air and small gardens preserve both their health and their morals they are now crowded into the town. The proximity of the market, and the convenience of public houses, are frequently the temptations which allure the poor; while an exorbitant rate of interest for money employed in the erection of such buildings is the inducement with the owners... Cottages with two or three confined rooms and without even a back door or common sewer, may be seen by those willing to gain information at the expense of their stomachs." However, this correspondent was more indignant that these cottages did not pay rates than at the fact that people should live in such squalor. This was very typical of early nineteenth century attitudes to poverty.

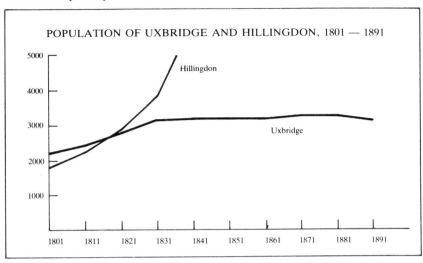

POPULATION OF UXBRIDGE AND HILLINGDON, 1801 — 1891

One effect of the rapid increase in population was a change in the tradesmen living in the town. Writing in the 1880's Giles Hutson says that there was a complete change in the fifty years from 1830. "A glance at the names over the shop fronts is to the old inhabitant more significant and more indicative of change than even the wholesale alterations in the fronts of shops and houses. Very few names are now to be found, the representatives of which were acting and energetic leaders of public local life and business then, almost all have passed away. The few, and there are not a score, are the names of descendants and are all that are to be recognised as having been to the front at that time. And not in any instance is the same person carrying on business now who did then: indeed as far as can be ascertained, there is no one left who was in business in Uxbridge in 1830, so complete is the revolution which has been effected in that space of time." That the nineteenth century was a period of change cannot be overstated and all aspects of life were affected.

INDUSTRY

At the beginning of the nineteenth century the most important industry in Uxbridge was the market and the mills connected with it. It was generally known as the largest pitched corn market in the country and the mills supplied London with the bulk of its flour. Giles Hutson has described the market at its peak in the 1830's. "Early in the morning, even by five or six o'clock, the farmers' waggons laden with corn for sale began to arrive. Many of these waggons came from a considerable distance, from Shepherds Bush, Willesden, Edgware, Hendon in that direction, from Staines, Hounslow, Hampton and other places along the banks of the Thames between Marlow and Kingston, whilst from the district around Rickmansworth many came, and from Chalfont, Wycombe, Amersham

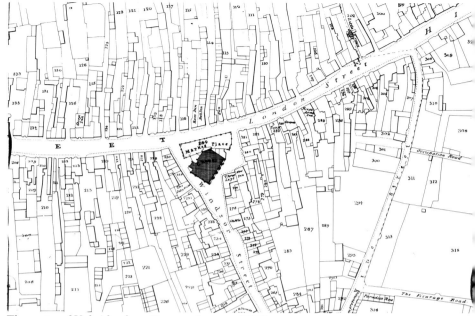

The centre of Uxbridge from Trumper's map of 1825.

and Missenden in Buckinghamshire, and even from the country about Chinnor in Oxfordshire, considerable quantities were brought.

"At eight o'clock the first Market bell was rung, when Lenten corn, that is oats, barley and other spring corn sown about the time of Lent, might be offered. It was against the rules of the Market for any corn to be sold before the ringing of this first bell and then only the kinds first named.

"As the morning advanced a larger number of waggons were constantly arriving loaded with wheat and all of it was pitched in the Market place, one sack upon another, if room for it could be found there, when if not it was placed in the gateways or on any other spare piece of ground in the immediate locality.

"The second bell was rung at twelve o'clock giving notice that the sale of wheat might commence. This prohibition of commencing sales before a given time was made to prevent any enterprising speculator, who had got a priority of news which ensured him prices would go up, stealthily buying up the corn before other dealers had arrived on the ground, and as twelve o'clock was the time agreed upon as suitable for commencing to sell wheat, the Millers and Dealers assembled at that hour and then a scene of great business activity ensued, which lasted about two hours, and during this space the greater part of the grain on offer usually changed hands.

"These sales were effected at this date more frequently by the farmer himself selling his corn to the Miller, although in some cases a middleman or salesman undertook to dispose of it and thus relieved the farmer of all the trouble of dealing.

"This practice gradually grew in favour, until very few growers sold their own corn, and this made room for a considerable number of salesmen as the Market was a very large one, indeed said at that time to be the largest pitched market in England, that is where the corn was brought in bulk for sale.

"The custom of the market authorities was to take one pint from each sack of corn as the toll and the quantity thus taken has been known to reach the large total of forty-three bushels, representing 2,752 sacks of wheat offered for sale and of a money value of £4,000, a very different state of things from the present aspect of affairs in the Market House, where for many consecutive months not a single sack is brought and but a comparatively small quantity sold by sample. Yet with this large supply brought to market there was not enough to keep all the mills going as the demand was considerably in excess of these 2,700 sacks, and was made up by cargoes sent down from London.

"The sales or business of the Market were carried out... in the alleys or passages formed by the mode of pitching the corn.

"In many respects the old plan of bringing corn in bulk for sale had its advantages as well as disadvantages. The advantage was to the Miller, that he saw the whole bulk of his purchase instead of sample only. To the farmer the disadvantage was that he suffered the loss of the toll and if on the day his corn was brought he could not obtain a fair price or what he considered a fair price, he had to take it back again or warehouse it until another market day came round, and this of course entailed considerable expense, and in the mean time the bulk was lessened frequently by pilferers, sometimes by accident and surely by rats.

"These disadvantages being so numerous, the plan of selling by sample at last superseded the old way, when it was found that as a rule bulks came in equal to sample and that convenient arrangements could be made for delivery without the inconvenient obligation of being at the Market with horses and men at a certain day and hour, these latter thus being freed and therefore at liberty to work on the farm.

"The decline of the corn market may be accounted for in many ways. Large tracts of the best land which formerly grew wheat are now used as Market Gardens and in other parts much that grew corn is now laid down as meadow and a considerable acreage has been built on; also a very large portion cut up into brickfields and more to form the lines of railway constructed in the district. Also upon the repeal of the Corn Laws, steam having become almost universally used, many mills were started in London and worked by steam power and not by water power as our mills were."

The development of the sale of corn by sample was recognised by the Lords in Trust in 1859 when the Corn Exchange was instituted. The room above the Market House was altered to provide a place for business, but it was too late to halt the Market's decline. Some years previously the volume of corn passing through the Market House had severely damaged its structure. Mr. Bassett, a corn dealer, had used the upper rooms to store his corn. On the night of August 23rd. 1851 the floor collapsed, injuring two men. The accident could have been much worse as the Market House was the recognised meeting place for men out drinking, and was often used by them for sleeping off the night's debauch. On this night a runaway horse had caused the men to leave the Market House, thereby avoiding any serious casualties.

Corn was not the only commodity sold at the Thursday market. When the farmer brought his corn in his wife would come too. At the beginning of the nineteenth century this was the only way in which household supplies could be obtained, although by the 1880's most shops would deliver an order within quite a wide area. On market day the town's many shops were supplemented by street stalls selling every imaginable item. In addition the corner between St. Margaret's and the Market House was set aside for the chicken and butter market and the corner opposite was used for the sale of vegetables. The general market was repeated on Saturdays.

In addition to the market, the Fairs were held four times a year. As the market declined so did the fairs, and they had ceased entirely by 1888. Luckily we have a very good description of the Fair held on September 29th (known as the Statute Fair) in the 1850's. It was written by Thomas Strutt in his reminiscences of his childhood, the unpublished *'Peregrinations of a Kiddy'*. "It is Statute Fair Day, 29th September, and the streets are full of people, all flocking in from surrounding districts. The High Street on this side is lined with covered stalls, here and there with a caravan behind. On these stalls are displayed all kinds of articles, toys, whips, canes, whistles, trumpets, crackers etc., but several display Gilded cocks and hens, ducks, nuts and cakes, composed of Gingerbread. Stalls for nuts and walnuts. These extend from the 'Grapes' Inn, (the site of the present, (1982) library), to below the 'Chequers' by permission of the shopkeepers. The famous stall with its big round tin canisters with tray tops and its tastily set out shelves principally for Gingerbread nuts, is attended by the Misses King from Brentford. Their black hair in long Victorian ringlets on each side of the face. Their pitch on each occasion is in front of Mr. John Rayner's the Chemists shop.

"The Market House is lined with similar stalls, many of them for supplying the inner man of those who can manage it — winkles, crayfish, oyster, mussels and other shellfish, fried fish and potatoes, also black puddings, saveloys and such like delicacies.

"Greens and other toy stalls. The crowds of Farmers and their wives interviewing serving men and maidens who stood in groups for the yearly hiring. The labourers denoting their profession by placing in their hat wisps of hay for haycutters and binders; thatchers by bunches of straw; Horse Keepers by knots of whipcord, Ploughmen, Hedgers and Ditchers by some other sign. The General Fair proper is held in Heaborns Mead, a large open field on the right of Cowley Road opposite Prospect Terrace extending down to the river. Generally Wombwells Menagerie. Moving Waxworks both with good outside bands of musicians. One or two circuses, swings and roundabouts, booths for giants, dwarfs, fat women, peep shows, noted boxers of the day — cocoanut shies, shooting galleries and so on, too diversified to mention, and crowds of people who all seem to enjoy it. In later years this part of the fair was held in the field surrounding the Wesleyan Chapel in New Windsor Street." The Statute Fair was the largest of the year; the first two fairs of the year were concerned primarily with the sale of cattle, sheep and horses. The cattle fairs were held in a large field along Harefield Road. They were attended by a great many people, particularly from London.

The decline of the Market and Fairs was caused by a large number of factors. Chief among these was the development of the railway through West Drayton, leaving Uxbridge isolated. Although a branch line was eventually opened in 1856 it was too late to stop the decay. The agricultural region from which Uxbridge drew its supplies was also changing. As Giles Hutson said, market gardens, brickmaking and building took over the farmland. The slow growth of suburbia, centred around the railway stations, made an agricultural market irrelevant.

At the height of Uxbridge's prosperity there were thirteen mills working in the area. Three of these were in the town, the rest within a short distance along the Colne and Frays. As Giles Hutson says, even the large amount of corn passing through Uxbridge market was not enough to sustain these mills and extra supplies had to be brought in from London, usually by canal. The men who owned the mills, particularly the Mercers and the Hulls, were very wealthy and were the leading families in the town. All the mills were conveniently close to the Grand Junction Canal; this made bulk transport of the milled flour cheap and easy. Frays Mill even had its own wharf. All the mills were water powered and were dependent to a certain extent on the weather; too much rain was as bad as too little. Technological advances combined with the decline of the market led to a corresponding decline in the milling industry in Uxbridge. By 1895 there were only four mills remaining on the Frays.

In 1806 an Act of Parliament was obtained which provided for the completion of paving the town (begun in 1785) and lighting it. Both paving and lighting were confined to the High Street and ended at the town boundary at the top of Vine Street. The lights used were oil lamps, which gave out only a feeble glimmer. No lights at this time were very bright. In rich houses expensive wax candles were used. In shops and cottages oil lamps and tallow candles were normal. The oils used were from vegetables and fish as petroleum oils were then unknown. In the early years of the nineteenth century Messrs. H. and D. Grainge experimented with gas lighting in their own workshops. This was so successful that they proposed lighting the town between the King's Arms and the White Horse, at London prices. In order to bring the price down the townspeople formed a committee which discussed the matter but did little else and for a while gas lighting was forgotten. In 1824 the British Gas Light Company applied to be allowed to light the town, but were refused permission by the Lords in Trust. In about 1832 James Stacey, a private speculator, constructed a gas works behind the Dolphin Public House on Uxbridge Moor. The High Street, shops and houses were then supplied with gas lighting. At an inauguration ceremony held in the Boys' Schoolroom over the Market House there was a display of a large star formed by jets of gas. To the unsophisticated townspeople this was very striking. The gas street lighting covered only those streets formerly lit by oil lamps. This continued until after 1854, when the newly formed Local Board of Health ordered that all public roads, and where possible alleyways, should be lighted. At first gas was not metered, but was charged at so much per light per year. Mr. Stacey would walk the streets at night and complain if he found anyone with a light on stronger than he thought it ought to be. Mr. Stacey was bought out by a few Uxbridge men and the company became known as the Uxbridge Old Gas Company. In 1854 John Hardy formed a new gas company, the Uxbridge and Hillingdon Consumers Company, in competition. For a time gas was cheap, but the new company bought up the old in 1861 and could then charge what it liked.

Apart from the market, one of the staple industries of Uxbridge had always been brewing. There were four breweries in the town by 1851, and five by 1866. Harman's brewery was in the High Street, at no. 180, and Heron's at no. 162. The Uxbridge Brewery was situated between Providence Chapel and the High Street, and this building later became the Uxbridge Steam Laundry. The Colne Brewery was behind Frays Mill, and at present (1982) is the premises of

High Street looking west c.1850

Hay-Lambert caramel manufacturers. Both these last two breweries were owned by the Mercer family. The Windsor Street Brewery, belonging to Grimsdale and Wells, was in Chapel Street near the top of New Windsor Street. The Windsor Street and Uxbridge breweries had closed by 1909. The last brewery to close was Harman's in 1964.

Associated with the breweries were the many inns and beerhouses. In 1853 there were fifty-four public houses in the town, of which twenty-four were in the High Street. By 1897 the number of inns in the town had decreased to forty-five and there were only seventeen in the High Street. There are now only four inns in the High Street. Drunkenness was a very serious problem in Uxbridge throughout the nineteenth century. The inns were open all day, except on Sundays when they were open from early morning until Churchtime at eleven o'clock. In the 1830's the sale of intoxicating liquor was forbidden until one o'clock on Sundays, which spared the churchgoers the sight of drunken brawls in the Market House.

The opening of the canal in 1796, with its cheap transport for heavy goods, provided the stimulus for the development of a new industry in the Uxbridge area. This was brickmaking. The area is very rich in the sort of clay suitable for making bricks, but until the canal was built their transport outside a purely local area was impossible. The first small brickfields to be worked were between Cowley and Yiewsley around 1815. By 1818, according to Redford and Riches, several hundred men were employed in them. The importance of the industry, particularly south of Uxbridge, grew rapidly. By 1856 over 240 acres in Hillingdon parish were being worked. They were said to be a great source of wealth to Uxbridge. One effect of the rapid growth of the brickfields was the influx of labourers. Brick making at that time was very labour-intensive; all the clay had to be dug, moulded and fired by hand. The labourers were better paid than the agricultural workers and spent a great deal of their money on drink. According to Giles Hutson "many of that very rough class of workman or labourer, the brickmaker and navvy, made a practice of visiting Uxbridge of Saturday evenings. Money with these men at that time, at least during the summer, was plentiful, and their love of beer being great, they indulged largely and scenes of riot and violence were often to be witnessed." The brickfields continued to expand until the 1880's. At that time the supplies of brick-earth were beginning to run out and the industry began to decline by the turn of the century. The last brickworks closed at Stockley in 1935.

The Grand Junction Canal provided the stimulus for many other new industries to develop in Uxbridge. Warehouses and wharves sprang up on Uxbridge Moor and at the west end of town; it became a centre for the redistribution of goods such as timber, slate and coal to the surrounding district. The Uxbridge Moor area was the centre for industrial development and by the 1850's there were a plate-glass mill, parchment works, oil mills and mustard mills as well as the gas works. The town also had some iron foundries. The oldest firm was Grainge, Rogers and Grainge who occupied premises off the High Street from about 1800. Stacey's Iron Works were built in George Street in the 1820's and employed about fifty men. The factory closed down shortly before 1900. The Albert Iron Works opened in 1862 in Murray's Yard, behind the Falcon Inn. All these foundries made agricultural implements. Despite these developments Uxbridge never grew into an industrial town. Its main disadvantage was in not being on a main railway line. Although the canal had stimulated developments in the early part of the century it was superseded by the railway and the canals themselves went into a decline. Uxbridge stagnated.

High Street looking east c.1850

The most important factor in the rise and fall of Uxbridge was transport. At the beginning of the nineteenth century the roads were the most important means of communication. The Oxford Road was very busy indeed. In the 1830's there were over eighty stage coaches a day passing through Uxbridge, as well as the vast number of private coaches, waggons, carts and other vehicles. Most of these were drawn by several horses, sometimes eight or more, and every inn yard in the town had large stables to accommodate them. Most of the corn and hay to feed these travellers' horses was supplied by the local villages, especially Hounslow and Denham. Some small carts were pulled by dogs, but they were often cruelly treated, and in 1839 this was forbidden by law. Much traffic also went on foot; that is, large herds of cattle and sheep were driven from their grazing grounds in Wales and the Midlands to market in London. At different times of the year the road would be crowded with labourers walking from one district to another in search of work; hay time and harvest were particularly busy.

At the beginning of the nineteenth century the only other method of transport was by water. The Grand Junction Canal had linked Uxbridge with the Thames at Brentford in 1794 and the through route to the Midlands and Leicester was open in the autumn of 1800. Most of the goods carried on the canal were heavy and bulky. Lysons, in his '*Historical account of those parishes in the County of Middlesex not described in the Environs of London*' (1800) lists the main goods carried to and from Uxbridge in 1799;

	tons		tons
Coals	6650¾	Bricks and tiles	131½
Grain	4968½	Stone	108
Flour	4612½	Coke	68¼
Sundries	1821½	Loam	49½
Ashes	1318¼	Timber	18
Manure	164	Lime	14¾
			19925½

Transport by canal was cheap but slow. A new technological development rapidly overtook both road and canal; this was the railway. In 1838 the line from Paddington to the west was opened with a station at West Drayton. The volume of traffic on both road and canal decreased rapidly. In Uxbridge the Cowley Road, leading to West Drayton, assumed a new importance and buildings began to appear along it. Between 1840 and 1842 William Tollit started an omnibus service, linking Uxbridge with the station. Several schemes were proposed to link Uxbridge with a railway. Finally, in 1853, work began on a branch line between Uxbridge and West Drayton. This opened with a station in Vine Street in 1856. The station attracted so much traffic that Vine Street had to be widened in 1859. This branch line was not entirely satisfactory, as it was only a single track and through passengers had to change trains at West Drayton; there were many abortive schemes to improve the situation. Uxbridge never regained its position as a major market town and there were no further improvements in the town's communications until the next century.

PUBLIC HEALTH AND LOCAL GOVERNMENT

At the beginning of the nineteenth century Uxbridge was a very dirty, unhealthy town. The piped water supply introduced in 1701 had been destroyed by the construction of the Grand Junction Canal. In 1800 the Lords in Trust ordered two deep wells to be sunk and others were dug privately or by subscription so that in the 1830's there were five public pumps working. This was very inadequate for a town the size of Uxbridge; many of the poorer people were nearly two-thirds of a mile's walk from the nearest fresh water.

  The main streets of Uxbridge were kept swept and watered during this period by the inmates of the Workhouse, who used for this purpose small water trucks filled at either the town pumps or in the River Frays. This gave the false impression that Uxbridge was a clean town. However, according to Giles Hutson, "with all this presumed cleanliness, abominations existed not now to be dreamed of." Down both sides of the High Street ran open square brick drains. By the 1880's these were used only for rainwater but in the 1830's they were the only method of drainage and sewage disposal. They had to cope with household waste, overflowing cesspools and other noxious sources. The yards leading from

Bell Yard just before its demolition in the 1930's

the High Street had only one open drain, down the centre of the yard, and these flowed into the main drain in the High Street. The Borough Ditch was also used as a cesspool. Attempts were made to deal with the sewage by having it collected by cart every morning, but this only added to the nuisance by leaving a bad smell in its wake for the rest of the day. The drains flowed directly into the Frays, thus polluting that river. Also many of the yard-dwellers kept pigs, often housing them in their cottages, and allowing them to roam at will over the town. This was finally forbidden in 1840.

The bad conditions of the cottages have already been described. Crowded together in every available spot, without drainage, badly built, with tiny rooms and only one door, these slums often held more than one family and were a perfect breeding ground for disease.

At the beginning of the nineteenth century there were no controls at all on any developments. The town was governed by eight men appointed by the Honor Court, a relic of medieval times. They were: two constables, four headboroughs and two ale-conners. After the Honor Court was dissolved in 1813 these officers were appointed by the church vestry. The Lords in Trust were interested in the provision for the poor and in improvements to the town, but they had no interest in improvements to the sanitation. It took serious outbreaks of cholera to change their minds.

The other major factor in the unhealthy condition of Uxbridge was the number of cemeteries in the town. There were three: those attached to St. Margaret's, to Providence Chapel and to the Quaker Meeting House. The first two were overfull and were believed to contaminate the water supply. In 1853, by Government order, these two cemeteries were closed for the sake of the public health. A Burial Board was formed which bought land off Kingston Lane as a new cemetery, which opened in 1856.

Disease was rife in Uxbridge. The death rate was very high, particularly among young children; over one third died before their fifth birthday and the average adult life-expectancy was only about thirty-two years and two months. It was cholera that finally spurred the townspeople into action. The disease first visited the town in 1831, brought by a tramp, but a cool autumn hampered the spread of the disease and Uxbridge was spared an epidemic. Cholera appeared again in 1849 and this time the epidemic was very severe. There was concern that sanitary reforms should be made and that a Local Board of Health should be set up. In April 1849 Uxbridge was the first town in England to petition Parliament for an enquiry under the newly enacted *'Public Health Act'*. As a result William Ranger, superintending inspector to the General Board of Health, visited the town, and made a report. Ranger found that the worst conditions, as expected, were in the yards where over a third of the town's population lived. Some yards, such as Chequers Yard, had no privy accommodation and all the yards were drained by open sewers. The improvements recommended by Ranger included the construction of reservoirs on Uxbridge Common, which would enable every house to have a supply of clean water. Also existing privies should be converted to water-closets and many extra ones provided. Tubular drains should be used and problems arising from overcrowding and poor ventilation tackled.

In September 1849 the Uxbridge Local Board of Health held its first meeting. It was under the superintendance of the General Board of Health and its duties included: "the more effective paving and supplying with water, lighting, drainage and otherwise cleansing the town. Power is vested in the Local Board to remove, or cause to be removed, all and every nuisance occasioned either by the accumulation of filth or foul and imperfect drainage. To seize and have destroyed all unwholesome meat, fish etc. exposed for public sale."

After this good beginning the sanitary reforms ran into trouble. There was much controversy about the jurisdiction of the Board and the expense of the proposals. The rate-payers felt it was a fine idea in principle, but they should not have to pay. It was not until 1853 that the boundary was finally agreed upon and there were always grumbles at the cost of the work. The completion of the drainage and water system was made much more difficult when people refused to sell their land. The Board was forced to lay its pipes below the roads and footpaths and the reservoir on Uxbridge Common had to be built under the road as one man objected to the sale of sixty-five square feet of the common. The waterworks in Waterloo Road were in operation by 1854.

Part of the 1848 Public Health Act provided for the appointment of a Medical Officer of Health. His duties were to advise on preventive measures rather than treatment of the sick. The General Board of Health found it difficult to define those duties, so it was not until 1854 that Thomas James was appointed Medical Officer of Health for Uxbridge. He held the post until his death in 1883, when he was succeeded by William Rayner, the Uxbridge chemist.

The new water supply proved inadequate for the increasing demand and had frequently to be turned off at night to conserve supplies. In 1889, to help the situation, the landlord of the Dolphin on Uxbridge Moor offered his deep well as an extra water source. The Rickmansworth Valley Water Company was formed in 1884, at first to serve only Rickmansworth, but in 1885 it was extended to cover an area as far as West Drayton and Hayes. In 1889 the Company laid its mains through the Uxbridge area, in return for which they supplied the town with water at a fixed rate. The Rickmansworth Valley Water Company took over the town's water supply in 1948, when it added Uxbridge to its name.

The main problem with drainage was the treatment and disposal of the sewage. The sewage works on Uxbridge Moor discharged its effluent into the Colne, and there were frequent complaints from landowners and the Thames Conservancy that the river was seriously polluted. It was not until 1894 that anything was done to alter the method of treatment.

By the end of the nineteenth century there had been enormous improvements in the standard of living of even the poorest inhabitants of Uxbridge. Although slums still existed in the town the general level of housing was much cleaner and healthier. Far fewer young children died and the average adult life-expectancy increased to forty-three years. People's attitudes had also changed and they now expected local government controls over buildings, drainage and other matters. In response to this changing attitude there were some important changes in local government, gradually leading to more control over all aspects of life.

The first changes in the government of the area came in 1827 when Uxbridge finally became a separate parish. In 1834 the Poor Law Amendment Act took the responsibility of caring for the poor away from the individual parishes, and instead several were grouped together as a Union. The Uxbridge Union covered much the same area as the present Hillingdon Borough. All the separate workhouses were closed and the paupers transferred to an enlarged Hillingdon Workhouse. This eventually formed the basis for the modern

Hillingdon Hospital. After the creation of the Local Board of Health in 1849 the next major change came in 1875 when the Local Board became an Urban Sanitary Authority, with responsibility for the township of Uxbridge, and a Rural Sanitary Authority was to have responsibility for the rest of the area covered by the Uxbridge Poor Law Union. In 1894 the Uxbridge Urban District Council was formed; it took over the duties of all the previous boards, which were dissolved. On the 1st of April, 1889, the Middlesex County Council was created.

Law and order were affected by the changes in local government. Since the Middle Ages the town's two constables had been responsible for keeping the peace, but by the nineteenth century they were very inadequate. In 1829 Sir Robert Peel set up the Metropolitan Police Force in London. This was so successful that other towns, including Uxbridge, decided to adopt a similar plan. According to Hutson there was at this time a great deal of drunkenness and many unsolved burglaries in Uxbridge. The constables and nightwatchmen were unable to cope. There were two nightwatchmen, each equipped with a lantern and a heavy stick. They walked the streets, calling out the time and the weather and often visiting public houses. Their noise gave thieves plenty of warning and they were seen as legitimate targets for drunken pranks. Hutson says "on one occasion the watchman, enclosed in his box, was laid with the door of the box downwards where he had ignominiously to remain until some person passed by who was willing to assist him to get on his legs again. This watchbox was somewhat similar but not so substantial as the sentry boxes which are placed about government offices for the soldier on duty to retire to when the weather is bad, and was chained to the iron railings outside the Old Bank." As the official law enforcement was so bad the local people formed themselves into societies to offer rewards and prosecute criminals, while several shopkeepers patrolled the streets themselves. The Uxbridge Volunteer Police Force was formed in 1836 and was housed in the recently vacated workhouse on Lynch Green. The force consisted of one sergeant and three men and was under the control of the town Watch Committee. However, in 1840 the Metropolitan Police area was extended to include Uxbridge and the local force was disbanded. The Metropolitan Police station covered Uxbridge and Hillingdon and was situated on the corner of the Uxbridge Road and Kingston Lane. In 1871 a new police station was built in Windsor Street and the Kingston Lane station closed.

One responsibility of the Local Board of Health not yet mentioned was the Uxbridge Volunteer Fire Brigade. This was formed in 1864. The station was in Windsor Street until 1909, when it moved to Cricketfield Road to make way for the new Post Office. In 1933 it moved to the former Empire Electric Cinema in Vine Street. All the men were volunteers, rather like the modern lifeboatmen; when the alarm sounded they would leave their businesses and run to the fire-station. They did not confine themselves to Uxbridge but were called upon by a very wide area around the town. Anyone who called out the Fire Brigade had to pay its expenses. The Volunteer Fire Brigade served the people of Uxbridge until the Second World War, when they were replaced by the full-time service of the London Fire Brigade.

EDUCATION

The nineteenth century saw the growing involvement of the state in education. At the turn of the century the two leading schools in Uxbridge were the Uxbridge Free School which had been founded in 1706 and was supported by the Lords in

Trust with the profits from the Market, and the Uxbridge School, a private school founded in 1790. In 1809 the Free School was reorganised under the Lancasterian system, where the older children helped to teach the younger. In 1816 the Girls' School of Industry was founded, based on the previous free school for girls which held its classes above the Market House. The girls were expected to pay for their education by their handicrafts, particularly sewing, the object being to turn out girls as suitable servants. In 1817 a new building was erected for the Girls' School in George Yard, where about eighty girls attended. In addition there were several small 'Dame' schools, where parents paid about fourpence a week for their children's rudimentary education. The education of the poor children of the town was very simple; they learnt little more than how to read and write and do simple arithmetic. It was not felt necessary for the lower classes to know any more in case they began to get ideas above their station in life.

In 1820 Cave House School was founded. This was a private school catering mainly for the sons of local tradesmen and was situated in a substantial house at the west end of the High Street. In 1850 the then headmaster, Robert Wilkinson, moved the school to Totteridge Park in Hertfordshire, but the premises were taken over by another school with the same name. In 1878 the Cave House School and Uxbridge School amalgamated, but the reputation of both schools had declined and although it continued for some years it was not so successful as formerly and finally closed in 1900.

By 1835 there were five day schools in Uxbridge; the British (formerly the Uxbridge Free School) School had 187 pupils, while 107 girls attended the School of Industry. The three other schools were small private affairs. There were also three girls' boarding schools as a counterpart to the boys' Uxbridge and Cave House Schools. In that year the British School and the School of Industry were reorganised. The boys' schoolroom over the Market House was now inadequate and new buildings were provided in the Cowley Road into which the boys moved in 1835. The profits from the market were no longer enough to support the school and in 1826 a charge of one penny a week was levied on each boy attending the school. This was increased to twopence in 1833 and in 1836 the school received its first grant from the Government. Despite financial difficulties throughout the century the school survived until 1928, when the pupils were transferred to the Greenway County School. The Cowley Road premises then became the town's first full-time rate supported library.

After 1835 several new schools were opened to meet the needs of the rising population. New Windsor Street Infants School was opened in 1839 and closed in 1911. It held between 140 and 170 pupils. In 1846 a school was erected on glebe land belonging to St. John's Church, Uxbridge Moor. It was known as the Uxbridge Moor National School and held 123 pupils. Although it was closely connected with the church, Religious Instruction was not compulsory. The school was finally closed as recently as 1980. Also in 1846 the Uxbridge Moor Ragged School opened. This was organised by the Waterloo Road Mission and was for the poor children of the district. By 1864 the school occupied the Meeting House with fifty-two pupils each paying twopence or a penny. All were taught reading and writing and the twelve oldest girls were also taught needlework. The school closed in 1892. St. Margaret's and St. Andrew's National Schools were built within a few years of each other, in 1864 and 1869. St. Margaret's infant department was added in 1869, by which time the school had 213 pupils. Many of these children had been bribed or otherwise persuaded to move from the British School. St. Andrew's

1868.

UXBRIDGE ALMANAC.

ADVERTISEMENTS.

CAVE HOUSE SCHOOLS,

UXBRIDGE.

PRINCIPAL—MR. J. HUNT, M.C.P., F.R.G.S.

Terms—From 25 to 35 Guineas per Annum.

Advertisement for Cave House School

School was built to serve the newly formed parish and to begin with had only fifty-five pupils, some of whom were taught writing and arithmetic, although all were taught to read. The school was extended in 1897.

The 1870 Education Act made the provision of education compulsory, although attendance was not. Where provision was inadequate it was to be remedied by local school boards. However, the town of Uxbridge was well supplied with schools run by voluntary societies and no new schools were needed. The Act also provided for increased financial help for the voluntary schools. Further acts were passed making elementary education compulsory and raising the school leaving age to twelve. Although the Government became more concerned nationally with the provision of education, the efforts of the voluntary bodies in Uxbridge made their intervention unnecessary.

Whilst many children attended school they learnt little more than how to read and write. As adults they often felt the need to improve on this lack of education. The nineteenth century was the great age of self-improvement. Despite long hard hours at work young men, and sometimes women, would often spend hours studying at night. Many schools held night classes and there were societies dedicated to educating working men.

The earliest educational societies in the town were confined to the middle and upper classes. The oldest of these was the Uxbridge Book Society, consisting of about sixty members of the nobility, gentry and clergy of the area. Another, similar, society was the Uxbridge Reading Society, formed in 1815. Both these societies had sizeable libraries open only to their members. In 1836 the Literary and Scientific Institution was formed and these two societies merged with it. The most important of the educational societies was the Uxbridge Young Men's Improvement Society. This was formed by two radical young men, John Bedford Leno and Gerald Massey, and other young men who wanted a literary society and reading room entirely unconnected with any religious or political party. The society was founded in 1845 with twenty-eight members; throughout its life membership averaged around eighty and it was still in existence in 1899. Classes and lectures were given in all sorts of subjects and discussion meetings were held. The society had a good library and subscribed to several newspapers. The society also produced its own newspapers, edited by Leno and Massey. These papers were *'The Attempt'*, *'The Uxbridge Pioneer'* and *'The Spirit of Freedom and Working Man's Vindicator'*; they were all full of very radical politics, the last most of all; it was nicknamed by one Uxbridge baker *'The Spirit of Mischief or Working Man's Window Breaker'*. After Leno and Massey went to London in 1850 to pursue their political careers the papers collapsed, but the Uxbridge Young Men's Improvement Society continued its work among the working men of the town.

RELIGION

There was little religious controversy in Uxbridge during the nineteenth century. Most activity was concerned with meeting the needs of an increasing population. In 1842 the Church of England finally recognised the importance of the town of Uxbridge when it ceased to be dependent upon the mother parish of Hillingdon and became a parish in its own right, with St. Margaret's as the parish church. The parish boundary followed that of the town. The rapid development of Uxbridge Moor led to the building of the church of St. John the Evangelist in 1838. In 1847 a Wesleyan Methodist chapel was built in New Windsor Street. Part of the great

Victorian religious revival was its evangelical nature: its supporters felt compelled to spread the word of God wherever they could. This accounted for the thousands of missionaries who went all round the world, especially India and Africa, to preach. Missionaries could also work closer to home. From about 1851 a gospel mission was organised in connection with the Uxbridge Moor Ragged School in Waterloo Road, which had opened in 1846. In 1864 a new building was opened with accommodation for the mission services, a reading room, day and Sunday schools. In the latter part of the nineteenth century the congregation declined and in 1892 the Ragged School closed.

Although the population of the town of Uxbridge remained fairly stable in the latter part of the nineteenth century, the area around the town developed considerably, particularly the area known as Hillingdon End. Therefore, in 1865, the parish of St. Andrew's was created and the church built. It was designed by Sir George Gilbert Scott, architect of St. Pancras Station, and built of local Cowley bricks.

Another Methodist congregation was formed in 1864. Their first chapel was in Chiltern View Road and is known as Burr Hall, but services were held in several places until a permanent chapel was opened in Lawn Road in 1876. Other non-conformist sects which met in Uxbridge included the Catholic Apostolic Church, which had a chapel in Montague Road from the 1850's until it was destroyed by a German bomb in 1940. There was a small Baptist community in Uxbridge from the 1930's. Meetings were held in cottages in Bonsey's Yard and then the Market House until they built their own chapel in George Street in 1856. This became known as Montague Hall. Shortly after this the congregation declined and the chapel closed. The Temperance movement was very strong in Uxbridge and the Blue Ribbon Gospel Temperance Mission met in the public rooms from 1884 until 1896. In 1887 the Uxbridge Salvation Army Corps was formed. It met first in premises in Bell Yard until 1899, when it moved to Montague Hall.

Throughout the nineteenth century Uxbridge continued its tradition of strong Protestant religious activity. There was no Roman Catholic activity until 1891, when the church of Our Lady of Lourdes and St. Michael was formed, although its premises in Lawn Road were not registered for worship until 1893.

In the Uxbridge churches, much energy went into rebuilding and renovating existing buildings. In 1818 the Quaker Meeting House was rebuilt, and this building still stands. In about 1820 the tower of St. Margaret's was completely rebuilt and at the same time the corner of the church was altered to widen Windsor Street. In approximately 1850 Providence Chapel was refronted in the fashionable neo-classical style. In 1872 the interior of St. Margaret's was thoroughly 'restored', when nearly all the windows were replaced. In 1882 a vestry was built on the site of the old chicken market. The next year the Old Meeting House was substantially enlarged, while still retaining much of the original building. The interior of Providence Chapel was renovated in 1890.

POLITICS

At the beginning of the nineteenth century, Uxbridge was still not separately represented in Parliament. The electors of Uxbridge had to vote for a representative for the whole county of Middlesex, and to cast their vote had to travel to the county town of Brentford. This was changed with the 1832 Reform Act, after which Uxbridge was one of the centres at which polling could take place. This Act also widened the franchise, so that any male person who owned or rented a house or land worth more than £12 a year was entitled to vote.

Before the 1832 Reform Act a day would be fixed for the election to start, but not for it to finish. As long as one elector per hour appeared the election continued. Voters would be brought to the poll and entertained at the expense of the candidate, electors were often bribed and other costs meant that an election was an expensive business for a candidate. After 1832 voting took place in several centres and lasted only two days. In Uxbridge the polling took place in the boys' schoolroom over the Market House. Giles Hutson has left us a vivid description of an early nineteenth century election, very different from the orderly affairs of today.

"At the upper end of the room the Sheriff with his clerks, agents and leading supporters of the candidates were stationed. On one side of the room a way was kept for the voters to pass up to give their votes at the head of the room, which having done they returned by a corresponding way on the other side of the room, or which was frequently the case joined a body of onlookers assembled in the middle of the room.

"This gathering was mostly of a very unpolished character, and as the voters passed up the room they were cheered or hissed according to the view the assembly took of their political tendency. They were chaffed or groaned at according to the side these rowdies had ranged themselves on; and anyone who had outraged public opinion, or who was thought to have done so, or who from any cause was unpopular with the non-voter was assailed with the most unpleasant and leading questions as to his honesty, extraction, circumstances, wife, son, daughter or anything that was his or any other matter likely to be offensive.

"There were men with a coarse sort of ready wit who laid themselves out or were employed by the agents of both political parties during the election and the names of George Bagley, Sam Powell and Mark Fisher will by some be recalled as the readiest, wittiest and most offensive of all.

"The interest taken in the County Elections immediately after the passing of the Reform Bill was very keen. The old inhabitant will remember that Lord Henley was put up on the Tory side but was not successful in ousting either George Byng or Mr. Joseph Hume, the other two candidates. After Lord Henley at another contested election Mr. Pownell was the chosen of the Tories and he also was unsuccessful but later Mr. Hume gave the greatest offence possible to the drink-selling people who had hitherto been his enthusiastic supporters by his advocacy of the movement which resulted in passing an act forbidding the opening of public houses until 1 o'clock p.m.; an act which perhaps more than any other ever passed led at once to a perceptible improvement in the habits of the lower class of working men — and in our own particular town to the stoppage of drunken riotous behaviour which had for so long scandalised the more steady-minded inhabitants. Again a Tory was put up, this time General Wood of Littleton, and as the publicans voted en-masse against Mr. Hume, the Tory candidate was returned. Shortly after, Mr. Byng, who had reached the distinction of being the oldest member of the House, died and his nephew was elected to the vacant seat which he held until he was removed to the House of Peers."

Uxbridge was involved in most of the political debates of the nineteenth century, in so far as many of the inhabitants took a keen interest in events. However, despite the efforts of John Bedford Leno there was little unrest even over the question of the 'Charter' which led to riots elsewhere in 1848. During the 'Swing' riots of 1830, caused by agricultural distress and the introduction of new machinery, there were riots in Iver but nothing happened in Uxbridge.

The people of Uxbridge continued to vote for members for Middlesex until 1884. In that year the Redistribution of Seats Act gave Uxbridge its own Member of Parliament. In the election of 1885 F. D. Dixon-Hartland, Conservative, was elected with 5093 votes, a majority of 2478 over his Liberal opponent, J. P. Rickman. He was returned unopposed in the election of 1886 and also in 1895 and 1900. He won comfortably in the 1892 election, but only scraped in with a majority of 145 in 1906. He was still the Member for Uxbridge when he died in 1909. In the twenty years from 1885 until 1906 the electorate increased enormously, from 9902 to 15936. This was partly a result of increased population, but mostly a consequence of a widened franchise, enabling more men to vote.

THE MILITARY

The first half of the nineteenth century saw much unrest throughout the country. The end of the Napoleonic Wars was followed by a severe economic depression which was blamed by many of the poorer people on the introduction of new machinery. In the agricultural areas particularly there was great distress and many people starved. In these circumstances bands of starving farm labourers, inflamed by political agitators under the leadership of the fictitious Captain Swing, met together to destroy farm machinery, burn hay ricks and perpetrate other outrages. These riots occurred all over England and came as close to Uxbridge as Iver. On December 1st, 1830, labourers at Iver and Shredding Green went around armed with cudgels and compelled householders to give them food, drink and money. This, understandably, alarmed the townspeople of Uxbridge, who feared that the rebellion might spread. On the 30th of December the Uxbridge Yeomanry Cavalry was re-formed. (As already mentioned, it had been originally formed in 1797 to meet the threat of invasion by the French, and was disbanded in 1801.) A Volunteer Infantry Corps was also formed.

The troop of cavalry was commanded by Charles Newdegate of Harefield Place, and after his death by Hubert de Burgh of Drayton Hall. All the officers were members of the leading families of the Uxbridge area. The members of the unit all had to provide their own horses and uniform. The uniform was dark green with black trousers. According to Giles Hutson, who obviously suffered in it, the suit was "anything but comfortable and nothing could have been designed more hideous as a military uniform."

The Corps was never called on to put down any rising by the agricultural workers, but some years after its formation there were fears that it might have been needed. In 1848, immediately following a revolution in France, the Chartists presented their petition to Parliament, demanding Parliamentary and electoral reforms, and great riots were feared. The Uxbridge Yeomanry were put on the alert to march if needed to back up the regular troops, which happily they were not. On this occasion the Corps was under the divisional command of the Duke of Wellington.

The Corps trained for eight days each year, when the men were paid by the Government. Pay was at first 3s 6d., but was raised to 7s 6d. in 1840. The training was regarded as a very pleasant social occasion. It began with a dinner to which the men invited the officers and ended with another where the officers

Uxbridge Yeomanry Cavalry uniform, 1879

invited the men. In between the men drilled on Uxbridge Common or on the estates belonging to the officers. On one occasion, during a drill on Uxbridge Common, the command was given to charge, but the officer forgot to order the men and horses to halt. Several soldiers jumped the ditch and hedge across Park Road and into Hillingdon House Park. One horse got stuck in the the middle of the hedge and several men fell off their horses.

The troop was often called for escort duty on Royal journeys. Its first attempt at this duty was not altogether successful. In 1834 the Uxbridge Yeomanry Cavalry escorted William IV on part of his journey between Windsor and Moor Park. The first part of the journey was accomplished successfully, but while the soldiers were awaiting the King at Moor Park they were liberally entertained. On the return journey, in high spirits, they got lost and took the King into a ploughed field. The Corps' last escort duty was performed in 1851 when they escorted Queen Victoria from Watford to Windsor. Even this was not without incident, as lacking orders to the contrary, the Queen was taken on a roundabout route through Uxbridge so that as many people as possible could see her.

The Corps at first consisted of eighty mounted men and eighteen officers, although by 1839 it had fallen to sixty-seven men, of whom three were officers. In about 1843 a brass band was formed at the expense of the officers. Also at about this date races were instituted with the aim of improving the quality of the troop's horses. The race course was laid out in the grounds of Harefield Place. (This is the house near Uxbridge, not the one in Harefield.) It was later moved to West Drayton. After the excitement of the Chartist riots in 1848 recruitment greatly increased and the Corps was divided into two troops. In 1871, as a result of the Franco-Prussian War, the Yeomanry Corps was enlarged and became known as the Middlesex Yeomanry Cavalry, with its headquarters still in Uxbridge. In 1877 the last training session was held in Uxbridge and from this date the Uxbridge connection was very slight.

At the same time as the Uxbridge Yeomanry Cavalry was formed the Uxbridge Volunteer Infantry was raised. This was more popular with the local tradesmen as it did not necessitate the possession of a good horse to join. The commandant was Thomas Hurry Riches. Training drills were held on Uxbridge Common and rifle practice in gravel pits along Harefield Road. The Infantry Corps was never called on for any military duty but often performed the service of protecting property after a fire. Mr. Riches retired as commander after twenty years and was succeeded by Count Peter de Salis of Dawley Court. Soon after, the interest in the Corps declined and it was disbanded.

During the 1830's the staff of the Royal West Middlesex Militia were stationed in Uxbridge. The depot consisted of non-commissioned officers who were trained to take charge of the regiment should it be called up. The men lived in Hillingdon End, opposite the entrance to the grounds of Hillingdon House. On Sundays the men would be preceded to their Church Parade by a band, which was much appreciated by most of the townspeople. The militia was raised by conscription. All males aged between eighteen and forty-five were eligible and the name would be drawn by ballot. Those who could afford to would pay another man to take their place. Militia Clubs were formed in which the members paid a small weekly sum and if called up the club would pay for their replacement. These clubs were made redundant in 1848 when the militia was reformed and voluntary enlistment became the method of recruitment. This reorganisation also saw the end of the West Middlesex Militia.

In June 1853 the Royal Elthorne Light Infantry Militia, under Col. F. W. Villiers, was raised in Uxbridge. The colours were presented by Lady Lumley on September 15th 1855, and later in the same month the regiment moved to Aldershot for training. The Militia transferred its headquarters to Hounslow in 1879. In 1881 the Royal Elthorne Light Infantry Militia was one of the regiments which united to form the Duke of Cambridge's Own (Middlesex Regiment). During its short stay in Uxbridge the regiment made a lasting impression on the area. The troops were in barracks off the Greenway, in Enfield Place; the name probably came from the rifle used. Some of the houses in the Greenway were built to house the officers, and the street names Elthorne Road and Villiers Street both commemorate the regiment, as does the public house, the Militia Canteen. The regiment's drill hall still stands in Whitehall Road and is now (1982) used as a Youth Centre.

SPORT

The kinds of sport enjoyed by the people of Uxbridge changed greatly during the nineteenth century. As the century progressed they became more refined, less brutal and more organised. Sports, in fact, are a very good example of the transition from eighteenth century to modern modes of thinking.

The sports enjoyed at the beginning of the century were the rustic and violent sort. Blood sports particularly were among the favourites. West Middlesex, with its newly enclosed fields and small hedges, was good foxhunting country and the Old Berkeley Hunt met frequently in the Uxbridge area. Stags were still hunted on Uxbridge Common as late at 1826. These sports were, of course, enjoyed only by the more wealthy townspeople. However, there were many other diversions to occupy the rest of the citizens. Hillingdon Fair in the 1830's was very popular with all the people of the area. Giles Hutson tells how the fair, held on May 16th, attracted the children and youth of the Uxbridge working classes. "The amusement consists of the usual assortment of shows and so-called rural sports. These were climbing the greasy pole, dipping the head in water for oranges or into flour for money, or eating rolls which had been dipped in treacle and being suspended from a bar with a piece of string, the operator with his hands tied behind him took his stand under the roll bobbing and snapping at it until it was consumed, the prize being awarded to the one who demolished the delectable morsel in the shortest time.

"Sport of a kind very much more cruel was also provided at this fair. It is just fifty years ago (1830) since the last public badger baiting took place and this was at the fair. This sport was peculiarly acceptable to that contingent supplied by the brickfields; those people employed in that line being but a short remove from the savage, but they were not alone in their liking for cruelty for many persons of a much higher grade in life sought such scenes with avidity, and on this occasion the badger was drawn by a dog belonging to a very opulent and prominent person."

Giles Hutson's remarks themselves show the difference in attitudes from one part of the century to the next. The Uxbridge Cricket Club's games and matches and the races organised by the Uxbridge Yeomanry Cavalry were very popular sporting occasions for both participants and spectators. In 1870 the Uxbridge Amateur Football Club was founded. Home matches were played on Uxbridge Common against local sides. In 1873 an Uxbridge player, Hubert Heron, played for England in the second international match against Scotland.

Heron played for England several times and in 1876 he and his brother Frederick became the only two brothers ever to appear in an international side and an F.A. Cup winning side in the same season. By this time they were both playing for the Wanderers. In the 1888-9 season Uxbridge won the West Middlesex Cup, which they won again in 1891, 92 and 93. In 1894 Uxbridge was one of the founder members of the Southern League Division Two. Also in 1894 the team won the Middlesex Senior Cup, which they regained in 1896. In 1898 Uxbridge reached the finals of the F.A. Amateur Cup but they were narrowly defeated by Middlesbrough, who then turned professional. During all these successes the team remained firmly based in Uxbridge; nearly all the first team players had been born within half a mile of the Market House. Despite their playing record, the club's expenses were not matched by its income, and in 1899 the financial position was so bad the club had to withdraw from the League and many players joined other clubs. Although the club soon revived it never attained its former status and remains today a local amateur club.

Other sports also became more popular as people had more leisure time and more money to spend. The Uxbridge Cycling Club was founded in 1890 and organised weekly meetings, cycle races, sports and gymkhanas. In 1892 the Hillingdon Golf Club was formed. Sports were also included as part of any celebration. The egg and spoon race and men's hundred yard dash were as much a part of the celebration of Queen Victoria's Golden Jubilee in 1887 and Diamond Jubilee in 1897 as were the fireworks and banquet.

ENTERTAINMENTS

During the nineteenth century the theatre was very popular with all levels of society. Uxbridge was no exception. The earliest performances in the town were put on by travelling troupes who performed in local barns. The town's first permanent theatre was built in 1820 by a Mrs. Burns and her sisters "in an enclosed field belonging to Mr. Allum near the bridge, Uxbridge." This came to be known as the Treaty House Theatre. The repertoire included the play *"Lovers' Vows"*, which caused so much trouble in Jane Austen's *'Mansfield Park'*. Many theatrical performances were spoiled by the rowdy nature of the audience, and Mrs. Burns and her sisters, according to their advertisements, were "determined to keep the admissions to the amusements perfectly select: so that visitors may enjoy their entertainment perfectly free from the intrusion of improper company." Visiting troupes also used this theatre, as well as large inn rooms, such as the Court Room at the George.

There were two improvised theatres in the town in the middle of the nineteenth century. The Windsor Street Theatre was in use in the 1830's and stood near the site of the present Post Office Sorting Office. Another site in Vine Street was used by travelling companies, first of all using tents; by 1849 this had developed into the Royal Prince of Wales Theatre. (It subsequently became the Empire Electric Cinema.) The town's only purpose-built theatre was the Theatre Royal in Chapel Street, opened in 1869 and in use until about 1914. The interior was "sumptuously" decorated in silver, gold and blue and held 365 people. Most of the plays performed here were melodramas. Parts of the building can still be seen, in use as a workshop.

Much of the entertainment enjoyed by the people of Victorian Uxbridge was not professionally produced, but performed by amateurs. Several of the large inns, particularly the George and the White Horse, had large

Windsor Street, showing the old almshouses before demolition in 1909

assembly rooms where all sorts of meetings were held. In 1837 the Public Rooms, or Town Hall, were built at the top of Vine Street. These rooms were used for lectures, concerts, and amateur dramatic performances. Groups such as the 'Uxbridge Blackbirds', who performed 'negro' entertainments, and school orchestras and choirs were the main sources of entertainment. In December, 1893, Gordon Craig, son of the actress Ellen Terry who had a weekend cottage in Uxbridge, made his first attempt at theatrical presentation at the Town Hall in an amateur production of Alfred de Musset's 'No trifling with Love'. He later became internationally famous for his revolutionary ideas on stage design. The Town Hall was later converted to a cinema, 'The Savoy', and is now (1982) a bingo hall.

In the main the social life of Uxbridge in the nineteenth century was limited to what people could provide for themselves. In 1853 a young woman, Emily Goldar Fearn, kept a diary. This was the year of her twenty-first birthday and she lived in Windsor Street with her mother, sister Cecile, step-father Henry Richardson Kingsbury and a step-brother and sister. Emily was a sociable girl and her diary is full of the events which made up her life, which was typical of most girls in Uxbridge at the time. A few days in January 1853 are representative of the way in which girls of the lower middle class occupied themselves:

"Wednesday, January 19th. Miss Pratt (dressmaker) at work here — a miserable

cold day. Considerable bargains to be had at the drapers Goodman and Noke who are dissolving partnership. Capital flowers at ½d. per spray, purchased several bunches.

January 20th. Rose at 9. Ironed all the morning. Finished Mrs. Inchbald's 'Simple Story' a present from Mr. Shoppee whilst in Ealing. Aunt Stillwell came in. Miss Lovell called — Miss Tapleys came to tea — invited us to their home tomorrow, George also if he comes. Ma, Miss Tapleys, Cis and children walked up to Hillingdon, I went to the Post Office and Mr. Dancer's — met Mr. Rayner — made Mama a morning cap — retired to rest at 12.

January 21st. Rose at half past 9 — made the beds so badly with Cecile that Ma made us do them over again. Made a batch of bread — Ma out of humour this morning — I managed to keep my temper — I know I am quietly provoking — must try to improve. George not come today — made Ma a black cap. Afternoon Cis and myself took tea and spent the evening at Cousin Tapley's — Ma came in evening — Mr. Brown came in to supper. Theatrical anecdotes enlivened the supper table — singing and music in the evening — scandal after supper. Retired at 11.

January 22nd. Walked round common with Ma and Cis — bought some images for the children, met Miss Tapleys, Ma angry with me for wearing my brown dress too tight. Cis went to see Mrs. Dix."

Emily did have more exciting evenings; balls, the theatre, concerts and lectures in the Public Rooms formed a large part of her social life. She also read a great deal, everything from radical political journals to love stories, and her hobbies included collecting almost everything she could — coins, flowers, and fossils — and keeping a pair of doves in the parlour. Emily describes one evening party in great detail:

"March 18th. An invitation from Mrs. Cosier to ask Cis and I to supper at 8 o'clock this evening. Wonder if Ma will allow us to go and if so what shall we wear? *Mamma soon settled that. Miss Pratt was quickly sent for to make up my plaid pink barège, one of the Goodman bargains, and I sent a note of thanks to Mrs. Cosier. We worked hard and Mamma sent to Hillingdon with the children in afternoon, then to Hedgecocks and bought us hair-ribbons and pink belts. By ½ past 8 the dress was finished so Miss Pratt walked up to Cosiers with us. We found Miss Lovell, Miss and Mrs. Spencer Homewood and Mr. Aldred assembled. A Miss Sweetall or Weetall also, who decidedly proved herself the young lady of the evening — also was very deaf — a little figure and very frenchified air — she was dressed in shaded silk with a net laying round her head and large knotted gold earrings — the Empress style.*

After raffling for some pocket books, which I unfortunately did not win, then Miss Weetall sang some Spanish songs to her guitar but with too much gesture to please me. After a sumptuous supper Miss Lovell and Miss Weetall played the piano by turns and we had a merry dance until 2 o'clock. Cis upset her plate in her lap at suppertime to the great amusement of all the company. Two tables joined for supper and Cis placed her plate between the two. Miss Weetall was too full of herself. I think her jokes were numerous, but not pointed, scarcely passable. Mrs. Cosier is a very nice woman — so fond of a romp and fun. Miss Carter, one of my horrors was there. A Mr. Bridges also. I had to drag him through the dance — reached home at ½ past 2."

The social life of nineteenth century Uxbridge as shown in Emily Fearn's diary differed very little from that shown in the Scott family letters of over seventy years before. This was the pattern for the whole nineteenth century; it took the advent of modern technology to change it.

Newspapers were a very important part of life in the nineteenth century as they were the only form of contact with the outside world. The first local newspaper to appear regularly in the town was *'Broadwater's Buckinghamshire Advertiser and Uxbridge Journal'*. This was printed in Amersham and covered a wide area of Buckinghamshire and West Middlesex from 1840 onwards. From 1860 this paper, now known simply as the *'Buckinghamshire Advertiser'* was printed in the King's Arms Yard, Uxbridge. In 1880 John King founded the *'Uxbridge Gazette'*. W. J. Hutchings had acquired the *'Advertiser'* in 1903 and the two papers ran in competition until 1919 when the two firms amalgamated to form King and Hutchings, which still produces the *'Buckinghamshire Advertiser'* and the *'Uxbridge Advertiser and Gazette'* as well as many other local newspapers as part of the large Westminster Press company. In the 1870's the town had two other papers, the *'Uxbridge Chronicle'* and the *'Uxbridge Marvel'*, as well as the *'Uxbridge Review'* in the 1890's, but none of these papers lasted.

As the nineteenth century progressed, the speed with which changes occurred rapidly increased, although the second half of the century saw the rate of change slow down and Uxbridge became left behind in the race towards the modern world. The town which saw the beginning of the twentieth century was vastly different from that of a hundred years earlier, but the changes which were to come were even more radical.

Chapter Six

Two World Wars

The dawn of the twentieth century found Uxbridge in a mood of quiet self-confidence. There was a feeling that nothing would ever change, least of all in Uxbridge. The town was a sleepy backwater, on no main transport routes, and although still a prosperous market centre its position as a major cornmarket had long since disappeared. The High Street was a mixture of well-to-do private dwellings and locally owned shops, although the yards and alleys behind were still appalling slums. People such as Cecil Sharp, the rediscoverer of English folk-song, lived in Uxbridge to escape from the busy life of London. Queen Victoria had been on the throne for sixty-three years, ruling an Empire that covered one fifth of the land surface and a quarter of the population of the world. However, all was not well in some parts of the Empire. In South Africa the Boer War had broken out in October 1899 and at first things had gone badly for the British. At the beginning of 1900 British troops were besieged in several towns, including Ladysmith and Mafeking. Several Uxbridge men were involved in the fighting. The tide of the war turned in the New Year and at the end of February Ladysmith was relieved. All over England people rejoiced at the news. In Uxbridge there was great excitement; flags were hung out, bells were rung and the Uxbridge Prize Band played patriotic songs. There was even more rejoicing in June when a grand carnival was held to celebrate the relief of Mafeking and the taking of Pretoria. The war dragged on for another two years, until May 1902, by which time much had changed in England.

On January 22nd 1901 Queen Victoria died, and the whole nation went into mourning; even the Uxbridge Gazette was printed with black borders. In Uxbridge most of the shops were shuttered, flags flew at half mast, the church bells tolled and the Uxbridge Prize Band played the Dead March from 'Saul'. On the 2nd of February the market was closed for the Queen's funeral. However, once people had recovered from the shock they began to look forward to the new reign, as the death of the Queen was seen as the end of an era, and for most people the twentieth century began in 1901. The new King, Edward VII, was proclaimed with great ceremony in Uxbridge by P. R. Smith, Chairman of the Uxbridge Rural District Council. The Coronation in 1902 was celebrated in the usual Uxbridge fashion with parades and sports on Uxbridge Common. In the next few years Uxbridge rapidly entered the modern world.

The chief causes of the transformation of Uxbridge were changes in transport. Within five years the town was no longer isolated. Probably the most important development was the extension of the Metropolitan Line railway from Harrow. Work began in 1901 and the line opened, with its terminus in Belmont Road, in June 1904. Uxbridge now had a fast and frequent service to the City. At first steam trains were used, but the line was electrified in January 1905. Another link with London was opened in June 1904 when the London United Tramways

Uxbridge High Street, 1910

Company extended its line from Southall to a terminus at the west end of Uxbridge High Street. The final link in the transport chain was made in 1907 when the Great Western Railway opened the High Street station, near the Treaty House. This line joined with the main London-Wycombe line near Denham. The company had plans to join its two stations at High Street and Vine Street; much of the land needed was purchased, but the plan came to nothing with the outbreak of war in 1914. Other developments in transport, the motor car and aeroplane, which were to prove significant in the development of Uxbridge, had as yet made no mark.

These rapid improvements in communications had a great effect on Uxbridge. The town became much more attractive to people for a variety of reasons. The frequent train services into the City meant that office workers could now live in what were still quiet rural surroundings and continue to work in London. Therefore a large number of new, middle-class houses sprang up within easy reach of the town centre. Many of these can be seen along the Cowley Road, the Greenway, Harefield Road and Lawn Road, around the edges of the old town centre. Uxbridge also became a tourist attraction for people living in Ealing and along the tram route. Although it may seem strange today, Uxbridge was regarded as an idyllic little country town to visit. On Sundays in summer the town would be crowded with families who would picnic at the Swan and Bottle and walk in the fields by the Colne.

During the early years of the twentieth century Uxbridge began to regenerate. Some new industries had come to the town towards the end of the nineteenth century and others came as the town became more accessible. In 1905 the Steel Barrel Company set up its premises in Rockingham Road. The grocery firm of Alfred Button set up a wholesale depot by the Belmont Road Metropolitan Line station. This has developed into the Budgen supermarket chain. One industry which was a great asset to the town, providing both jobs and beauty, was the flower nurseries. Before the First World War there were about six nurseries around the town but the largest and most important of these was Lowe and Shawyers off Kingston Lane. The firm had begun in 1864 when Joseph Lowe grew flowers in his back garden. By 1897 he owned several acres off Kingston Lane, specialising in growing roses and chrysanthemums. In that year, due to ill-health, Joseph Lowe took George Shawyer into partnership. By 1906, when a private company was formed, the firm was expanding rapidly and by 1914, with over 300 employees, it was the largest employer in the district. During the War vegetables replaced flowers and women replaced men workers. During the 1920's and 30's the business kept expanding. Nearly 200 acres were cultivated with a workforce of nearly 1000 and the firm was the largest cut flower nursery in the country. During the Second World War vegetables once more replaced flowers. Labour problems and cheap overseas competition after the War caused the decline of the business, which closed in 1958. Joseph Lowe died in 1929 and George Shawyer in 1943. Their memorial was the inclusion of their chrysanthemums in the Uxbridge Borough coat of arms.

In 1906 the water supply to the town was improved when a castellated water tower was erected on Uxbridge Common. The year 1907 was a very busy one in Uxbridge. As well as the new railway station, the new courthouse in Harefield Road was opened. Also in 1907 the Uxbridge County School opened in the Greenway. It was the first state secondary school in the town. This followed the passing of the 1902 Education Act which created a national system of primary and secondary education. The old School Boards were abolished and were replaced by Local Education Authorities based on the county. In 1928 the school moved to the Rectory House in Hillingdon and became Bishopshalt Grammar School, while the Greenway premises were occupied by the Greenway County Secondary School. Also in 1907 all the Uxbridge charities were brought together as the Uxbridge United Charities. They immediately began to build new almshouses off New Windsor Street, now known as Woodbridge House to commemorate the long association of the Woodbridge family with the charities. The old almshouses were demolished and replaced by the town's first purpose built Post Office, completed in 1909. In 1911 Whitehall Road Infant School, Cowley Road, was opened.

The modern world was rapidly catching up with Uxbridge. The Uxbridge and District Electricity Supply Company set up business in Waterloo Road, and by 1902 most of the town was connected to the supply. However, even as late as 1912 new houses supplied with gas lighting were still being built. In 1909 the town's first cinema, Rockingham Hall in the Lynch, opened, followed in the next year by the Empire Electric in Vine Street, opposite the station. The Empire closed in 1932 and the building was used as a Fire Station. Young people were also changing their amusements. In 1908 the town's first Boy Scout troop was formed in a garden shed in Chiltern View Road, only a year after the movement first began. This was also the year when great excitement was caused by the Olympic marathon competitors running through the town on their way from Windsor to London.

In November 1909 Sir Frederick Dixon-Hartland, the long-standing Member of Parliament for Uxbridge, died. Due to a political crisis Parliament was dissolved in December, and in the General Election of January 1910 the new Member for Uxbridge was the Hon. Charles T. Mills. The eldest son of Lord Hillingdon of Hillingdon Court, he was a very popular local figure. He was killed fighting in France in 1915 and was replaced by his brother, the Hon. A. R. Mills, who was elected unopposed. The suffragettes had their supporters in Uxbridge, but they were not very militant. They held lectures and concerts to support their cause of Votes for Women, but they did not indulge in such activities as breaking windows.

In August 1914 England was at war with Germany. By the time war was declared no-one was very surprised. The first reaction in Uxbridge was an immediate panic to stock up with food. An Emergency War Committee was set up which had the responsibility for ensuring food supplies and co-ordinating other aspects of the war effort at home. The army requisitioned several horses from local traders, which was seen as reasonable as trade was expected to decline during the emergency. Those men in the army reserves were called up and many others joined up straight away. The Uxbridge Gazette was reduced in size to save paper and football matches were cancelled. One of the effects of so many men joining the army was that their jobs were taken over by women. For the first time women were able to show that they could do a man's job, and do it well. Besides the men being gone, the war affected Uxbridge in many smaller ways; there were food shortages and rationing and soldiers were often billeted in the town. The reports in the Gazette of men killed or missing in action grew depressingly longer and in 1915 the whole town was saddened at the death of its M.P.

In 1915* the Cox family sold the Hillingdon House estate to the Government. It was used as a hospital and convalescent home for the Canadian army. Then in 1917 the newly-formed Royal Flying Corps took the place over as their Armament and Gunnery School. The peace of Uxbridge was shattered as the crews practised firing their guns. Other changes occurred as more buildings were erected in the park of Hillingdon House to accommodate the men. The Royal Flying Corps became the Royal Air Force in the following year.

In 1920 the R.A.F. Central Band made its headquarters at Uxbridge. In 1922 Aircraftman John Hume Ross enlisted at Uxbridge, where he spent three months' initial training. He was actually the famous T.E. Lawrence 'of Arabia'. His book *'The Mint'* is a graphic account of the short time he spent in Uxbridge.

The First World War finally came to an end in 1918. All day people in Uxbridge had been waiting for the news, and when a notice confirming the signing of the armistice on the 11th of November went up in the Gazette office window the town went wild. Flags appeared, people cheered, the artillery guns at Hillingdon House fired and the church bells rang. Workmen and schoolchildren were given a half-day's holiday and complete strangers kissed each other in the street. Even heavy rain could not dampen their enthusiasm and the rejoicing went

---

* So V.C.H. vol. 4, p.62: but a conveyance (GHA/DP 2378) discovered June 1982 in the possession of L. B. of Hillingdon records the sale of Hillingdon House estate (1) by the exors. of Col. Cox to the Cavendish Land Co., 26 May 1915 and (2) by the C.L.C. to the War Dept., 21 March 1918. The occupiers 1915-18 must therefore have leased or rented the property.

Peace Memorial and Methodist Central Hall in 1968

on all night, while the trains to London were packed with people going to join the celebrations there.

Immediately after the Armistice was signed Parliament was dissolved. The following election, the first since 1910, was the first in which women were allowed to vote. The Hon. A.R. Mills did not stand again and the new M.P. for Uxbridge was the Hon. S. Peel, a Coalition Conservative candidate, who defeated the first-ever Labour Party candidate for Uxbridge.

In July 1919 the official peace celebrations were held. Those in Uxbridge followed the pattern of most of the rest of the country. The occasion began with the ringing of the church bells. There were fancy dress parades and sports on the Common with tea for the children, followed by dancing. The day ended with a torchlight procession round the town by demobilised soldiers and sailors, culminating in a bonfire and fireworks. The opportunity was also taken to christen the newly-acquired motor fire-engine. In 1924, on Armistice Sunday, the memorial to the men of Uxbridge who fought and fell in the War was unveiled by the Dowager Lady Hillingdon, mother of Charles Mills. The memorial was situated outside the St. Andrew's Gate of the R.A.F. camp at Hillingdon House. It was moved to the Old Burial Ground in the early 1970's to make room for road improvements.

The land the soldiers came back to was not what they had been promised. They had been promised a land fit for heroes to live in, but nothing had changed. The war severely disrupted the economy and many industries were in decline. The slums were still there, as were poverty and disease. Women, having once escaped from the home, would never return entirely to their pre-war subservient role and they were now competing with the men for jobs. In Uxbridge the problems were not too severe. Firms in the town, such as the Steel Barrel Company, had done well out of the war and other new firms came to the town. The most important of these was the Bell Punch Company which set up its works in a disused mill on the Colne in 1919. This firm was to be one of the chief industrial employers in the town, manufacturing ticket-punching machines and other technical equipment. In 1921 Sandersons opened their wallpaper and fabric printing factory on the Uxbridge border. This is their centre for worldwide distribution. Motor cars and the telephone had come to stay, creating new jobs and altering traditional ones.

The Uxbridge Urban District Council realised the problems facing the town and set about a programme of improvements. One of their first acts was to acquire land no longer needed by the Great Western Railway's abandoned scheme to link High Street and Vine Street stations. This land was laid out as Rockingham Recreation Ground. The Council also concerned itself with housing and in the twenty years between 1919 and 1939 several council housing estates were built, particularly on Uxbridge Moor and in the area between the Greenway and the London Road. During the 1930's there was large-scale slum clearance in the High Street. During this time most of the yards were demolished and their inhabitants rehoused on the new estates. The town acquired another recreation ground in 1926 when Mrs. Kate Fassnidge gave a large part of her garden bordering the River Frays to the town as a memorial to her husband.

There were changes in the High Street. Many of the old established firms closed and were replaced by modern chain stores, such as Woolworths. In 1921 the Town Hall closed and was rebuilt as the Savoy cinema. In the same year the town's first bus services began on a route from High Wycombe to Uxbridge operated by the Thames Valley Company. In 1922 a bus garage for Uxbridge was opened just over the border in Denham, and the service rapidly improved. Also in 1922 the town's first free public library opened. This was housed in a former private house at the west end of the High Street and staffed entirely by volunteers; it had been accommodated in a baker's shop for a short while before the house was available. There was much new school building in 1928. Whitehall Infants' School was extended, which allowed the closure of the nearby Cowley Road Boys' School and St. Margaret's Infant School as their pupils were transferred. The Girls' School of Industry became Belmont Road Infants' School. In 1930 the library moved into the former Cowley Road Boys' School; it was now opened as a full-time branch of the Middlesex County Libraries and run by a professional librarian, Miss E.J. Humphreys. In 1931 a new Methodist Central Hall was built on the corner of Park Road. Private schools still flourished in Uxbridge and in 1926 Frays College opened in Harefield Road; George Orwell taught here for two terms in 1934 before catching pneumonia and being transferred to the Uxbridge Cottage Hospital further up Harefield Road. (The Cottage Hospital had been founded in 1868 and moved to Harefield Road in 1914.)

As communications of all types improved, Uxbridge became less isolated from national events. The General Strike of 1926 illustrates this. The strike was called for midnight on the 3rd of May and from that time there were no buses, trams or trains running. Coal was rationed and milk, meat and vegetables immediately increased in price. Some Uxbridge factories were affected, but in many of them the workmen stayed overnight so as to be able to carry on working. Train and bus services were soon resumed, staffed by volunteers. Meanwhile the townspeople gathered outside Randall's store in Vine Street to hear the news on the radio (few homes had their own sets yet). The Uxbridge shopkeepers were not very happy with the strike, as it occurred in the middle of a 'Buy British Empire Goods' promotional week and their sales were hit. The strike ended on the 12th of May, with no serious consequences for the town of Uxbridge as a whole.

In 1929 the local government of the area was reorganised. The Uxbridge Rural District Council was abolished and the Urban District Council extended to take in Cowley, Hillingdon, Harefield and Ickenham. The Middlesex County Council took over responsibility for the Union Workhouse in Hillingdon. They closed the workhouse and turned the buildings into Hillingdon Hospital.

During the 1930's the rate of change rapidly increased. For most of the people in Uxbridge life was much better than it had ever been. Wages were higher and hours of work shorter, so people could spend more time on leisure pursuits. Most houses now had a radio and the favourite entertainment was the cinema. On Boxing Day 1931 the Regal Cinema opened in the High Street and later the Odeon was built at the west end of the High Street. The cinema in the R.A.F. camp was open to the public, so the people of Uxbridge had a choice of four cinemas. In 1932 the Uxbridge Show, which had begun as a small horticultural event in 1909, was enlarged to include other events and soon began to attract large crowds annually. Except for a short break during the Second World War, the show has been an annual event ever since. It became known as the Hillingdon Show in 1965, when the new borough was created. As well as providing a 'fun' day out the show gave local people the chance to show off their gardening and handicraft skills. A popular summertime pursuit was swimming. There were recognised bathing stations along the Frays and Colne, but these were rather unsafe because of pollution; they were also rather primitive and not very deep. In 1935 the big new Uxbridge Open Air Swimming Pool was opened on land belonging to the former Hillingdon House Farm. In 1931 a new Roman Catholic church was built in Basset Road and the Lawn Road premises vacated.

As a result of better wages and increased leisure many families were now acquiring a motor car. In consequence Uxbridge began to suffer severely from traffic congestion. The Western Avenue, most of which was opened in 1934, was built to divert traffic from the old Oxford Road. As it finished at the junction with Long Lane it did not keep the traffic away from Uxbridge town centre. The last part, to link with the Oxford Road, was completed shortly before the outbreak of war. In the town attempts were made to relieve the problems by replacing the trams with trolleybuses in 1936. In 1937 the old narrow High Bridge and canal bridge were rebuilt. Increased use also meant that the old Belmont Road station was now inadequate, as in 1933 Piccadilly Line trains began to run through to Uxbridge. As part of the slum clearance programme Bell Yard was demolished and a new Metropolitan and Piccadilly Line station opened on the site in 1938. This station was one of a series designed by Charles Holden and the interior includes heraldic stained glass windows by Erwin Bossanyi. With its semi-circular forecourt facing the Market House, it gave the town a focal point it had not had before. The face of the High Street was changing as many shopfronts were replaced by more modern ones. At the east end of the High Street the Uxbridge Urban District Council decided to build new offices to replace the

Uxbridge Underground station in 1939

converted houses they were using. The large modern County Buildings included council offices, a library and museum and a health clinic. They were completed just as war broke out in 1939.

The emergency services had been preparing all through the summer of 1939 and they were ready for the air-raid sirens which sounded as soon as war was declared. Cinemas and schools were closed immediately, but the cinemas reopened after a week and the schools soon after that. A blackout was imposed and air-raid shelters were built throughout the town; the main public shelter was in Laundry Yard, but Government-issued "Anderson" shelters were provided for people to erect in their own back gardens. As the war progressed "Morrison" shelters were issued which could be used inside the house; one young boy found they were just right as a base for his model train set! Newspapers were reduced in size to save paper and strict censorship was imposed on all the news they carried. Gas masks were distributed and food rationing introduced. High Street station was closed to passenger traffic. The most immediate result of the declaration of war was a sudden rush of weddings. The new council offices were taken over as Air Raid Precautions headquarters, although the library did manage to move in. Throughout the war years there were bad accidents at night as people could not see in the blackout, and many were fined for showing a light which could have been seen by an enemy aircraft.

In August and September 1940 the area was bombed and two Uxbridge A.R.P. wardens were awarded the George Medal for rescuing people from damaged buildings. The centre of town was not hit, but houses in Rockingham Parade and Montague Road were damaged, the Catholic Apostolic

Church in Montague Road was demolished and several people were killed. In one incident people were killed when they were hit by machine-gun bullets from an R.A.F. plane which was chasing a German bomber. This was during the Battle of Britain, when we were losing many planes and pilots in action. The people of Uxbridge tried to raise enough money, £5,000 to buy a Spitfire. Although only £3,500 was raised this was gratefully received by the Air Ministry.

This period saw the R.A.F. camp at Hillingdon House at its busiest. Uxbridge was the control centre for No. 11 Fighter Group. The movements of enemy aircraft were plotted from information sent from radar stations and observers all through the South-East. The various fighter squadrons were then told where and when to intercept the enemy. During the Battle of Britain Winston Churchill visited the operations room several times and it was here that he is reputed to have said "Never in the field of human conflict was so much owed by so many to so few".

Most new development work in the town had stopped with the outbreak of war. Two projects, however, were finished. The junction of Vine Street and the High Street was widened in 1940 and in 1941 St. John's Isolation Hospital, founded in 1883, was extended. The builders of the hospital were congratulated on being able to finish the job under very difficult circumstances.

Rationing of most things was very strict. Food especially was very short and it was often difficult to cook a nice meal with what was available. Therefore, in 1941, a Food Advice Centre opened in the High Street to give advice on how to make the rations stretch further and taste more palatable. Also in 1941, in the old Waterloo Road Mission, a British Restaurant opened. This was run by the Uxbridge Urban District Council and the Ministry of Food and aimed to provide a good meal for 10d. (4p.).

The Second World War affected the people at home much more than any other war had done before. Although there was food rationing and bombing during the First War it was not on the scale of that from 1939-45. People were encouraged to do everything they could to help the war effort. A 'Dig for Victory' campaign encouraged people to grow their own vegetables, and many new allotments were made available by the Council. There were appeals for salvage; old saucepans and iron railings could be made into armaments. Funds were raised by voluntary efforts to help pay for munitions and in 1942 Uxbridge adopted H.M.S. Intrepid. Money was raised to help pay towards her cost and comforts were sent to the sailors on board. Most of the younger able-bodied men were away fighting. Those who could not go were encouraged to join the Civil Defence units at home. The Home Guard, Air Raid Precautions and Auxiliary Fire Service were all staffed by volunteers. As part of the emergency organisation the local fire brigades were centrally controlled under the London Fire Brigade and the Uxbridge Volunteer Fire Brigade ceased to exist as a separate entity in 1941.

The war finally came to an end in 1945. The news of peace was eagerly awaited and when it was finally announced over the radio there were great celebrations. The church bells rang for the first time since 1939 and the streets were decorated with flags. There were many street parties and the dancing went on late into the night. A special memorial service was held in St. Margaret's and the congregation overflowed into the Market House, where the service was relayed by loudspeaker.

Even before the peace had been signed plans were being made for the future. A General Election was called in July as a result of which Britain had its first Labour Government. Even Uxbridge, which had been solidly Conservative, elected its first Labour M.P., Frank Beswick, by a very narrow margin. Before the election the Paliamentary constituencies had been changed and Uxbridge was enlarged to include Ruislip and Northwood. The Uxbridge Urban District Council had been discussing plans for the site of the old sewage works off Cowley Mill Road. They had wanted to build a housing estate, but decided this was not suitable, so an industrial estate was planned. This was officially opened in 1946 and now has over fifty firms engaged mostly in light engineering.

Life gradually returned to normal as the men began to return from the fighting or from prison camps in Europe and the Far East. Many were so badly affected by their experiences, both mentally and physically, that their lives would never be the same again. Rationing was still in force as the country tried to recover and people felt very depressed as it seemed things would never improve. The very hard winter of 1947 did not help, coupled as it was with a severe shortage of fuel. However, there was a bright spot at the end of the year when Princess Elizabeth married Prince Philip. The Olympic Games provided some much-needed excitement in 1948. The Games were held at Wembley and the Torch passed through Uxbridge on its way there. The competitors were housed at R.A.F. Uxbridge, which was specially vacated for them. For a while it was commonplace to see famous athletes training on the local roads and to hear strange accents in the shops.

In the General Election of 1950 the constituencies were altered once again, and Ruislip and Northwood were separated from Uxbridge. Frank Beswick, the Labour candidate, was re-elected, as he was in the subsequent elections of 1951 and 1955.

The building industry was starting to recover after the wartime restrictions and there were several housing developments along the edge of town. The Swakeleys Road area was developed by the local firm of W. S. Try. Part of their development area included the Gospel Oak, a tree which marked the boundary between Uxbridge and Ickenham. Instead of felling the tree both it and its site were presented to the Council.

In 1951 the Festival of Britain was held on the South Bank site in London. A great many local people took advantage of excursion rail fares to visit the exhibition and for those who stayed at home Uxbridge provided its own small festival. There were special church services, local groups performed plays and concerts and there was a special shopping week and an Uxbridge Industrial Exhibition. However, more important for the future of the town, the Middlesex Development Plan was published. This provided an overall scheme for the whole county; certain areas were zoned for industry, others for housing. The plan laid down that Uxbridge should have more houses and shops but no new industry, and should be surrounded by Green Belt land. Also in 1951 the Uxbridge District Council decided to petition the Government to make Uxbridge into a borough. Their reasons were many and various and are best set out in their own words from the petition;

"Your petitioners believe that the granting of a Charter of Incorporation would tend to the great advantage of the District and to the promotion of its interests, by giving it a higher and more efficient form of Local Government and ensuring the stability of its institutions, by fostering public spirit and encouraging the more willing and efficient performance of public duties both by the inhabitants at large and by their

elected representatives, by encouraging the carrying out of measures for the further development of the District, and by giving to the District additional dignity, status and influence thereby enabling it to obtain that position among the Municipal Boroughs of the Kingdom to which its traditions, its growing wealth and advancement, large and increasing population and its enterprise, would appear justly to entitle it".

The discussions as to whether the charter should be granted went on for several years.

1952 was a year of change. A minor one was the introduction of zebra crossings in the High Street. At first both pedestrians and motorists were confused as to their use. The year also saw the death of King George VI. People were sad as he had been held in great affection. All the shops were closed during his funeral and several local memorial services were held. However, the accession of a new young Queen was seen as the advent of a new era. The New Elizabethans saw their future as one of progress. They were certainly right in that the next quarter century saw more changes in Uxbridge than in the rest of the century, if change can be equated with progress.

Chapter Seven

The Modern World

Queen Elizabeth II was crowned on June 2nd 1953. All over the country, including in Uxbridge, people celebrated with street parties. The ceremony was televised live from Westminster Abbey and this was the impetus many people needed to acquire their own television set. For those who did not have access to their own or a neighbour's set, a large one was placed in St. Margaret's Church where many people spent the whole day.

Television was not the only amenity of modern life to become generally available in 1953. The first hint of a drastic change in shopping habits was given when the Express Dairy opened Uxbridge's first supermarket at 22 High Street. The idea of self-service and pre-packaged food was so strange to the Uxbridge housewives that they had to be told how to use the shop. Rationing of most foodstuffs had ended, and in that year petrol rationing also ceased and petrol with brand names returned to the pumps. Another sign of returning normality was the reappearance of chocolate machines on the station, from where they had been removed in 1939. Uxbridge Magistrates' Court was extended and work began on a new telephone exchange in the grounds of the former Cave House School. The exchange was opened in December 1955 and made a big difference to telephone users. They could now dial many numbers directly without the assistance of the operator. Although 1953 marked the beginning of many things it also marked the end of one of the most important industries in the history of Uxbridge. Fountain's Mill, the town's last cornmill, closed down. It was bought by Glaxo for use as laboratories, but was severely damaged by fire in May 1954, and later became used as a Youth Training Workshop.

In May 1955 the Borough Charter was finally granted. It was presented by the Duchess of Kent at a grand ceremony at the Regal Cinema. Large crowds gathered outside to cheer, including the children who were given the day off from school. The charter was accepted by Councillor James Cochrane, Charter Mayor and last Chairman of the Uxbridge Urban District Council. He was made the first Freeman of the new Borough of Uxbridge in 1956 and died shortly afterwards. In 1958 the first new block of flats in the Council's post-war slum clearance programme was opened and named after him.

By the mid-1950's building had recovered from the wartime stringencies. Several new buildings were erected in Uxbridge, notably the Government offices in Bakers Road, Colham House, opened in 1956, and also, more importantly, plans were being made for a wholesale redevelopment of the entire town centre, including a new Town Hall. From 1959, when the plans were first mooted, until the late 1960's, when work finally began, the redevelopment of Uxbridge had an adverse effect on the town. As properties fell vacant they remained unoccupied until the part of the town from Windsor Street to the High Bridge was almost derelict. It gave the whole town a very seedy and run-down appearance. Throughout the 1960's Uxbridge had the air of a dying town as more and more firms and facilities closed down. In 1962, as a sign of the times, the Savoy Cinema closed and reopened as a bingo hall. Also in that year both Harman's brewery and Vine Street station closed and both their sites were earmarked for redevelopment. The tracks for Vine Street station were torn up in 1965. In the same year the Steel Barrel Company closed — and in the following year the even older established firm of Osborne Stevens closed its timber yard on the canal. The site of this was immediately redeveloped as the Highbridge Industrial Estate.

However, the 1960's also saw the opening of many new facilities and new developments in all directions. As the decade opened trolleybuses were replaced by the ordinary bus, although the poles to carry their wires were only removed in 1981. Uxbridge could not remain immune from the issues of the modern world and in 1962 the first of the Campaign for Nuclear Disarmament marches from Aldermaston to London arrived in Uxbridge on Easter Sunday. The marchers spent the night in Uxbridge, staying with supporters or sleeping on the floor of the Friends' Meeting House, much to the alarm of some of the inhabitants who were wary of what the 'beatniks' might get up to. For several years after this the annual march stopped overnight in Uxbridge, until it almost came to be anticipated. In 1963 work was begun on a new Hillingdon Hospital, completed in 1967, although the old hospital was still used and even part of the old workhouse was left standing.

By this time the reorganisation of the local government of London was being planned. It was the most drastic the area had ever seen. The old county of Middlesex was abolished and replaced by London Boroughs. Thirty-two London Boroughs were created to cover the whole area of the capital. Some of these Boroughs were related to older administrative areas and in the Uxbridge district the old Councils of Uxbridge Borough, Ruislip-Northwood Urban District, Hayes and Harlington Urban District and Yiewsley and West Drayton Urban District were combined to form one borough. There was much discussion about the name to be given to this new area, the parts of which had very little in common with each other, and there was some rivalry among the component parts as to the name to be chosen. One name greatly favoured was "Queensborough", as it was at Heathrow Airport, within the new area, that Queen Elizabeth II first set foot on English soil as Queen. Happily this was rejected in favour of 'Hillingdon', which was chosen as being the name of the most central place in the borough. The new borough was inaugurated in April 1965 with very little ceremony and less celebration. A relay race was held to mark the boundaries of the new borough and the Uxbridge town crier read the proclamation in all the areas concerned. Two major problems facing the new borough were its lack of any recognisable centre and a severe shortage of office accommodation. With these in mind the plans for the redevelopment of the Uxbridge town centre were finally approved, which now included plans for a new Civic Centre to house all the Council's services. Cllr. Mrs. Winifred Pomeroy, second wife of Walter Pomeroy who had been the first Mayor in 1955, was the last Mayor of the Borough of Uxbridge in 1964. She was Mayor of Hillingdon in 1973, providing a link with the past.

The detailed proposals for the new Uxbridge town centre were first put forward in November 1963, although they were not approved until 1965. This was the first time in the town's history that there had been planning on such a scale. Indeed, this was the first time that any real thought had been put behind the plan of the town centre; it had grown up naturally, meeting the needs of the town, and later builders had followed the status quo. By the early 1960's the nature of Uxbridge had changed considerably. It was no longer a rural market town but a shopping and business centre serving a large suburban area. The functions of many of the buildings on the High Street had radically altered and the yards particularly were no longer viable in their old form. They were too long and narrow and often with awkward access through narrow archways; many of them were semi-derelict, wasting much valuable land. A major factor in the need for a new town centre was the vast increase in road traffic and there was an increasing problem of lack of parking space. A combination of these and other reasons led the then Uxbridge Borough to decide on a comprehensive redevelopment plan, which was carried through by the London Borough of Hillingdon. The work was expected to take twenty years.

The redevelopment area coincided almost exactly with the old town boundaries. The area was divided into blocks which were designated as being for shopping, commercial or residential use and an outline of new roads was drawn. Although there have been some alterations to the detail of the proposals this is still basically the plan being followed today. The first part of the plan to be put into operation was the building of the new relief road and the area known as Block 1.

Uxbridge shopping precinct in 1973, before completion

The relief road was designed to divert traffic from the High Street, which would be pedestrianised, and to improve access to Cowley Road and New Windsor Street. From the High Bridge the new road went through part of the old Colne Brewery and the Odeon Cinema car park. A roundabout was built behind the Odeon to provide access to Harefield Road and the new buidings; this meant that in 1968 Fassnidge Hall, the old people's day centre, had to be moved to make way for the new road and most of the beautiful old gardens of the Cedars destroyed. Houses in Basset Road, Lawn Road and the Lynch were demolished and they all had their access to the High Street cut off. In designing the 'Vine Street Gyratory System' the Council reluctantly decided that the whole of Cross Street must be demolished. As this was one of the most attractive parts of old Uxbridge this decision must always be regretted. The original plan was to demolish most of Vine Street to widen the road, but when Vine Street station was closed it was decided to use the line of the old railway tracks instead, cutting across the cricket field to rejoin the High Street at a new roundabout at the junction with Park Road, on the site of the Eight Bells public house. The St. Andrew's Lodge of Hillingdon House was demolished and a new gate to the R.A.F. camp had to be built, while the Peace Memorial was moved to a new position in the Old Burial Ground. Work on this end of the road began in 1970 and was completed in 1974.

The Block 1 development was the largest block on the plan and was the first to be started and completed. This comprised the area along the High Street from Windsor Street to Harefield Road and bounded to the rear by the new relief road. Within this area everything was demolished except the Roman Catholic Church, the telephone exchange and the frontages along the High Street from near Old Bank House to Harefield Road. Everything else was felt to be too old or obsolescent to be worth preserving. Even Providence Church was demolished. Behind the more traditional shop-lined High Street the planners took the opportunity to provide two squares surrounded by shops. One was named Chequers Square after the old inn that formerly stood on the site and the other Market Square, where the market is held on Friday and Saturday. Above the shops were built multi-storey offices, flats and car parks. The whole thing was designed in a very modern style using grey concrete, and looking rather like a pile of child's building bricks. The first part of the precinct was open in late 1970 and the entire complex in 1972. Shortly after this the High Street from Windsor Street to Belmont Road was closed to traffic and paved right across. At the same time work began on Block 9, the area between the High Street, Bakers Road and Belmont Road. Here too new shops and offices were built. All this development necessarily meant the disappearance of many old Uxbridge shops, such as Kirby the ironmonger, Vernon Brown the seed and corn merchant and Rayner the chemist.

In 1962 the Old Meeting and Providence Congregational Churches merged to become the Uxbridge Congregational Church, meeting at the Old Meeting House. The two Methodist congregations from Lawn Road and the Central Hall had merged in 1957, using the Central Hall as their meeting place. In 1972 the Congregationalists, now known as the United Reformed Church, and the Methodists merged. They had a new church built on a site off Belmont Road, which opened in September 1972. With its distinctive pyramid roof Christ Church is a landmark of the new Uxbridge. Its modern design includes facilities for the headquarters of the Uxbridge Samaritans and the Hillingdon Association of Voluntary Services. The former Lawn Road Methodist Church was taken over by

Hillingdon Civic Centre in 1980

the Christian Scientists, while the Central Hall remains derelict (1982). A new Salvation Army citadel was built in Cowley Road, on the site of the old Cowley Road Boys' School, in 1974.

The next stage in the transformation of Uxbridge began in 1973 with the preparation of the site for the new Civic Centre. This was to be on the site of the old Council offices. Work began on the demolition of the Council offices in the summer of 1973. The library was still in residence and for nearly two years life was very difficult for both staff and visitors as they had to pick their way in through a building site and contend with the dirt and noise. Eventually, in 1974 the library moved to its present (1982) temporary building, the former Express Dairy supermarket. The new Civic Centre was designed to bring all the Council's departments together, thus resulting in a more economical use of manpower, as well as a saving on the rents of buildings leased to house various departments around the borough. Enough of the building was completed for staff to move in in late 1976, although it was not officially opened until April 1979. The design of the building is very controversial. It is a complete contrast to the stark concrete of the shopping precinct, being built in brick and tiles (over a concrete frame). It was designed by the architects Robert Matthew, Johnson-Marshall and Partners to harmonise with its suburban environment. Architects see it as a significant development in twentieth century architecture and it is an important building in its own right, apart from its function as the administrative centre of the London Borough of Hillingdon.

The next stage in the development of the town centre began in 1979 as work started on a new bus station and office block in Bakers Road, opened in 1983. Work started on the Block 8 site early in 1982. This site covers the High Street from the Station to George Street and as far back as York Road. A tall, American style, glass office block has been built here. Work started on the Block 3 site in 1983 with the demolition of the sixteenth century timber-framed building of Burge and Gall. In the triangle bounded by Windsor Street, the High Street and Vine Street it is intended to build another huge office block and a new central library. When this is completed the High Street and Windsor Street will be closed to traffic.

Now, nearly twenty years after their inception, the plans for a new Uxbridge are nearing completion. In that time the face and nature of the town have been radically altered. Many people who have not visited the town for some time have trouble recognising it. However, attitudes have altered since the early days. Now wholesale demolition for its own sake is not approved of and the idea

Map of Uxbridge in 1982

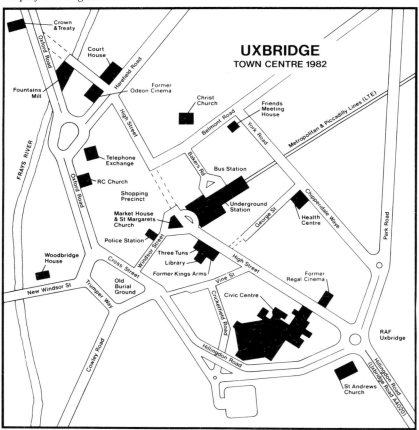

of conservation areas is gaining ground. In Uxbridge the whole of Windsor Street and the High Street from Windsor Street to Vine Street have been made a conservation area to try and preserve some part of the atmosphere of old Uxbridge. Whether this succeeds when huge office blocks are built right behind the old buildings is a matter for discussion. Another development is the restoration and re-use of old buildings, exemplified by the old Barclay's Bank, which has been gutted and rebuilt, keeping only the original facade.

In the meantime, while the building went on, the normal activities of the town continued. In 1965 there were significant educational developments in Uxbridge. First the Vine Street Youth Workshop opened in the former fire-station. This was intended to provide young people with practical experience in all kinds of technical and mechanical work. In September 1965 the first students enrolled at Uxbridge Technical College. At this college students could study for G.C.E. examinations not taken at school or study commercial or technical subjects in preparation for work. The technical college was officially opened by Anthony Crosland, the Minister for Education, in 1966. 1966 also marked a significant point in the history of education in Uxbridge as the first students started at the new Brunel University. During the rapid university expansion of the 1960's several Colleges of Advanced Technology were advanced to university status. One of these was Brunel C.A.T. at Acton, which was already in need of new buildings. With the closure of Lowe and Shawyer's nursery a large area of building land was available and this was acquired for the new university in 1963. The university, which offers courses mainly in technical subjects, was named Brunel after the great engineer and was officially opened in 1968. In 1974, the private school, Frays College, where George Orwell had briefly taught, closed. It was taken over by Hillingdon Borough and is now an Adult Education Centre. In 1968 the Belmont Road Infants' School, which had formerly been the Girls' School of Industry, was closed and superseded by the new Hermitage School in Belmont Road. This was named after a large house which had once stood along Belmont Road.

In the General Election of 1959 the longstanding Labour M.P., Frank Beswick, was defeated by Charles Curran, a Conservative candidate. In 1964 Frank Beswick was made a life peer. Mr. Curran remained the M.P. for Uxbridge until his death in 1972, except for a short period from 1966-70 when he was defeated in the 1966 election by the Labour candidate, J. C. Ryan. The current (1982) Conservative M.P., Michael Shersby, won the by-election which followed Mr. Curran's death in 1972.

Many national events closely affected the lives of the people of Uxbridge in the 1970's. In 1977 Queen Elizabeth II celebrated twenty-five years on the throne. There were many celebrations, including a great many street parties, and everywhere was decorated with flags and bunting.

In the same year the Regal Cinema closed. The building is listed as being of architectural importance and there are plans to convert it to a bingo hall. The economic recession has meant that many spending cuts have had to be made. One of these was the closure of the Uxbridge Cottage Hospital in 1978. At first this was merely for renovation, but its future has not yet been decided. In May 1979 Lord Hailsham, the Lord Chancellor, opened the new extension to Uxbridge Magistrates' Court. Businesses have found times very hard and some of the shops in Uxbridge have had to close, including two of the large new supermarkets, which both shut their doors in 1980 though they were soon replaced by other firms. 1980 saw Uxbridge Library celebrate its Golden Jubilee. 1981 opened with a frightening reminder of the modern world when an I.R.A. bomb exploded in R.A.F. Uxbridge on January 8th. One man was slightly injured and it brought the fear of terrorism very close to home. However, after this the nation was cheered with the news of the engagement of Prince Charles to Lady Diana Spencer and their wedding in July was the excuse for another round of street parties.

The appearance of the town has changed more in the last twenty years than it had in the previous 2,000. There is still much left to be done; approaching the High Street from the east the dilapidated appearance of the derelict Methodist Central Hall almost adjoining the boarded-up entrance to the Regal Cinema gives a depressing aspect. The backs of many of the shops and inns remaining in the High Street are broken down and unsightly, However, plans are in being for the redevelopment and improvement of most of these eyesores.

On the positive side, Uxbridge has regained much of its ancient influence over a wide area. It is a regional shopping centre of growing importance; it is the seat of Local Government and the administrative centre for the municipal services of the London Borough of Hillingdon; it has a long-established R.A.F. station of international renown; it is a university town with the staff and students of Brunel university making welcome contributions to community life; the Magistrates and County Courts are accommodated in a fine suite of buildings and their cases are often the subject of world news; there are firms of international repute and flourishing industrial estates providing a sound economic basis for employment; it has a major newpaper printing house; it is a public transport interchange and underground railway terminus.

Despite all the modern buildings and roads which have so altered the face of Uxbridge one can still see attractive reminders of the old town. The Market House and St. Margaret's Church provide the focal point for the High Street and behind them Windsor Street retains the charm of a bygone age. Some of the old inns remain to dispense hospitality to townsfolk and visitors alike as they have done throughout the centuries.

The town of Uxbridge has had a long history and it still remains a town and not a suburb. Indeed, it comes as a shock to many residents to find themselves living in Greater London and to hear Uxbridge referred to as "a town on the western edge of Greater London"; but it is the people who live in it and the events which have affected them that I have tried to depict. For those who live here now a knowledge of the history of their town helps to give them roots, a necessary thing in the modern world; while an understanding of the past can illuminate the future.

Select Bibliography

Printed works

ANGLO-SAXON CHRONICLE	
CAMDEN, William	Britannia. (1695)
CHAMBERLAIN, J.	Queen Elizabeth's progresses. (1821)
COLLINS, Desmond	Early man in West Middlesex. H.M.S.O., (1978)
FAULKNER, A. H.	Grand Junction Canal. David and Charles, (1972)
FOXE, John	Book of martyrs. (1554)
GOVER, J., MAWER, A. and STENTON, F. M.	Place names of Middlesex. (C.U.P., 1942)
GRIFFITHS, D. M.	A history of Uxbridge Cricket Club. (1971)
JARVIS, L. D.	Free church history of Uxbridge. (1953)
LELAND, John	The itinerary, (c.1538)
LYSONS, Daniel	An historical account of those parishes in the county of Middlesex which are not described in the Environs of London. (1800)
MIDDLESEX AND BUCKINGHAMSHIRE ADVERTISER & GAZETTE	1854-1982.
MIDDLESEX COUNTY RECORDS SOCIETY	Middlesex County Records, edited by J. C. Jeaffreson. Old series, 1549-1688. (1887)
PEARCE, K. R.	Old Meeting Congregational Church, Uxbridge, 1662-1962. (1962)
PEARCE, K. R.	Short history of the town of Uxbridge. (1970)
REDFORD, G. and RICHES, T. H.	History of the ancient town and borough of Uxbridge. (1818)
ROBBINS, M.	Middlesex. (Collins, 1953)
STONHAM, C. and FREEMAN, B.	Historical records of the Middlesex Yeomanry 1797-1927. (1930)
TROTT, Celia	The story of the Uxbridge Quakers from 1658. (1970)
UXBRIDGE BOROUGH COUNCIL	Town centre redevelopment. (1963)
UXBRIDGE LOCAL HISTORY AND ARCHIVES SOCIETY	Uxbridge Record. (1964-1981)
UXBRIDGE URBAN DISTRICT COUNCIL	Charter day programme. (1955)
VIATORES	Roman roads in the south-east Midlands. (Gollancz, 1964)
VICTORIA HISTORY OF THE COUNTY OF MIDDLESEX	vols. 1-6, (1911-1980)

Manuscripts

BLAKE, J.	A study of the growth and changes of industry related to improvements in communications in the Uxbridge area. (1979)
CATTLE, J. T.	The fight for Uxbridge's market tolls. (1939)
DAWICK, J.	The provision of education in Uxbridge in the nineteenth century. (1976)

DELL, E. R.   The economic fortunes of Uxbridge, 1500-1780. (1980)

FEARN, Emily Goldar   Diary. (1853)

FULKER, J. M.   A history of Uxbridge town in the County of Middlesex, 1800-1850. (1969)

HUMPHREYS, C.   Leisure and entertainment in Uxbridge and Ruislip and their neighbourhoods in the nineteenth century. (1979)

HUTSON, Giles   Recollections of Uxbridge. (c.1884)

PEARCE, K. R.   The railways of Uxbridge. (1971)

SCOTT, James   Letters to his daughter Nancy Norton. (1780)

STRUTT, Thomas   Peregrinations of a kiddy. (c.1873)

TIDY, S.   A century of public health reform in Uxbridge, 1800-1894. (1973)

WEARE, F. W.   The changing social and economic geography of the lower Colne Valley, 1781-1911. (1977)

Index

Page numbers in **bold** type refer to illustrations

94